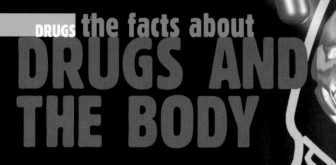

DRUGS the facts about

DRUGS AND
THE BODY

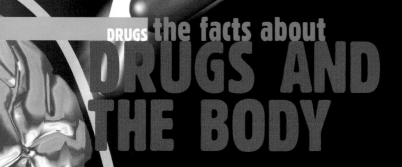

DRUGS the facts about

DRUGS AND THE BODY

LORRIE KLOSTERMAN

Marshall Cavendish
Benchmark
New York

Acknowledgment:
Thanks to John M. Roll, Ph.D, Director, Washington Institute for Mental Illness Research and
Training, Washington State University, for his expert review of this manuscript.

Marshall Cavendish Benchmark
99 White Plains Road
Tarrytown, NY 10591
www.marshallcavendish.us

Library of Congress Cataloging-in-Publication Data

Klosterman, Lorrie.
The Facts About Drugs and the Body / by Lorrie Klosterman.
p. cm. — (Drugs)
Includes bibliographical references and index.
ISBN-13: 978-0-7614-2675-2
1. Drugs—Physiological effect—Juvenile literature. 2. Psychotropic
drugs—Physiological effect—Juvenile literature. 3. Substance
abuse—Juvenile literature. I. Title. II. Series.

RM301.17.K56 2006
615'.1—dc22
2007002260

Medical illustration on page 19: Ian Worpole
Photo research by Joan Meisel

The photographs in this book are used by the courtesy of:
Cover photo: Alfred Pasieka/Photo Researchers, Inc.
Alamy: 14, Mikael Karlsson; 29, EuroStyle Graphics; 32, Kevin A. Somerville/Phototake
Inc.; 54, Phototake Inc.; 66, David Hoffman Photo Library; 68, Steve Allen; 99, INSADCO
Photography; 112, Dennis MacDonald; Photo Researchers, Inc.: 1, Alfred Pasieka; 6, Simon
Fraser; 26, M. Kulyk; 77, Arthur Glauberman; 86, Cordelia Molloy; 104, Bill Longcore

Publisher: Michelle Bisson
Art Director: Anahid Hamparian
Series Designer: Sonia Chaghatzbanian

Printed in Malaysia
1 3 5 6 4 2

CONTENTS

1 The Body on Drugs   7

2 Drugs and the
Nervous System   27

3 Drugs and the
Cardiovascular System   55

4 Drugs and the
Respiratory System   69

5 Drugs and the
Digestive System   87

6 Drugs and the
Reproductive System   105

Drug Table   120
Glossary   122
Notes   125
Further Information   128
Bibliography   130
Index   134

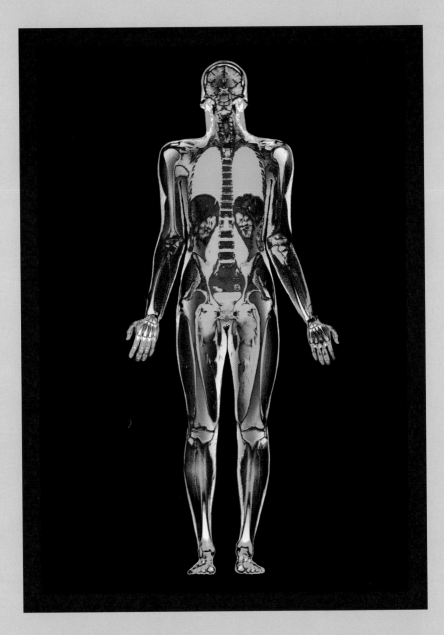

DRUGS ALTER THE FUNCTIONS OF THE BODY'S MAJOR SYSTEMS, WHICH INCLUDE THE NERVOUS, CARDIOVASCULAR, RESPIRATORY, DIGESTIVE, AND REPRODUCTIVE SYSTEMS.

1 THE BODY ON DRUGS

A drug is a chemical substance that alters physical or mental states. This simple definition describes what we observe when we see someone who has drunk too much alcohol or has taken cough medicine. But what is going on *inside* at the cellular level? What actually happens when the chemical substances in illegal and legal drugs flow through the bloodstream and reach the body's organs? Dazzling advances in cellular biology, biochemistry, and imaging technology in recent decades now make it possible for scientists to see what processes are going on "in there" when someone stumbles after too much drinking or gets drowsy after taking cough medicine.

But before those effects take place, the drug must enter the body. That happens through a route of entry. Nearly every drug relies on the body's network of blood vessels, or vasculature, to carry it to places where it will have an effect.

The mouth is the most common entry point for drugs. Numerous drugs come in solid or tablet form to be taken by mouth, then swallowed. Drug makers have designed many legal drugs, such as pain relievers, sleeping pills, and allergy medications, to be taken orally. A drug that is swallowed dissolves in the stomach and/or intestine and crosses into the tiny blood vessels—capillaries—that course through those organs. Once inside capillaries, a drug is swept along in the bloodstream and carried throughout the body.

Thin layers of cells that line the nose or mouth absorb certain other drugs—nasal sprays, sniffed cocaine, and nicotine in chewing tobacco, for example. Marijuana users and cigarette smokers inhale smoke into the lungs. There, such drugs easily move across thin cellular layers into nearby capillaries.

The skin is another entry route for certain drugs. Examples include acne medications, which users apply as lotions or creams, and skin treatments to reduce the itch of a rash or insect bites. These medications act on the skin itself and occasionally the tissues just below it. Drug makers design other drugs to penetrate the skin, enter the bloodstream, and reach other parts of the body, including the brain. Examples include stick-on patches containing nicotine or motion sickness medications.

The most direct drug entry route into the bloodstream is by injection into a vein (the intravenous, or IV, route). Doctors administer many legal medications this way, including anesthesia and the painkiller morphine. Within moments, the bloodstream carries such medications everywhere in the body. Injection is one of the main ways that users of heroin, cocaine, and amphetamines take illegal drugs. Sometimes drugs are injected into layers of skin or into muscle rather than into a vein.

Certain drugs lend themselves to multiple entry routes. A cocaine user, for example, may sniff, or snort, smoke, swallow, or inject it. Nicotine users may smoke cigarettes or chew tobacco.

Entry points influence the speed at which a drug takes effect. Oral ingestion of a drug is usually the slowest. Food in the stomach or intestines may obstruct the drug route or soak up some of the drug. Injection of a drug into skin or muscle also slows down a drug's effect since the drug slowly works its way through tissues before it reaches capillaries. Sniffing and inhaling cause rapid effects because drugs easily penetrate cellular layers in the nose and lungs and cross into underlying capillaries. Intravenous injection is another fast entry route. The faster a drug enters the bloodstream, the stronger its effects. IV drug users report feeling a "rush" because the entire drug dose enters the bloodstream at once.

From Bloodstream to Site of Action

Psychoactive drugs, including stimulants, depressants, hallucinogens, and antidepressants, influence mood, behavior, judgment, perceptions, alertness, reasoning, and other mental processes.

The brain has a system of special capillaries, the blood-brain barrier, that protects the brain from many viruses, bacteria, toxins, and other harmful substances. Psychoactive drugs, however, do cross the blood-brain barrier. Many of them do this by mimicking chemicals that the body naturally produces.

Mechanism of Action

The whole-body effects of many drugs are obvious—for example, the slurred speech and clumsiness during alcohol intoxication. Those effects are the result of changes that we cannot see—changes that occur at a microscopic cellular level. On that much smaller scale, the way in which a drug influences cells is called the drug's mechanism of action. A single drug may have many different mechanisms of action. The drug may also act on many different kinds of cells. Some general mechanisms of action may:

- **slow or block a cell's normal activities**
- **speed up or increase a cell's normal activities**
- **change a cell's activities so they are no longer normal**
- **temporarily damage or kill a cell**

A vast amount of scientific research is directed at understanding a drug's mechanism of action. Knowledge of a drug's mechanism of action is also important in providing effective treatment plans for drug users who are trying to overcome their substance abuse patterns. Research into various drugs' mechanisms of action has revealed entirely new information about the body. While studying why opiates, heroin, and morphine had such strong influence on drug users, researchers discovered the naturally occurring substances called endorphins. Experts now recognize that endorphins are important brain chemicals that help control a person's mood, pain perception, and more.

Many drugs influence cells because they resemble an endogenous chemical, one the body already produces. Morphine, amphetamines, cocaine, anabolic steroids, and THC (the active ingredient in marijuana), all have some similarity to natural chemicals in the central nervous system.

Drugs that resemble naturally occurring chemicals are similar enough to attach to or get inside a cell and change its workings. In some cases, the drug's effects depend on higher concentrations than would occur naturally.

Dopamine is a natural brain chemical with many different functions, depending on the part of the brain where it is released. Groups of dopamine-releasing neurons are key participants in an area of the brain called the pleasure circuit. This area is activated during enjoyable situations. Many psychoactive drugs boost dopamine levels in the brain which, along with other neurochemical changes, result in a pleasurable experience.

The illicit drug methamphetamine is an example of a drug that contains dangerously high quantities of a chemical that resembles a natural one in the brain. Methamphetamine is shuttled inside brain neurons just as the natural brain chemical dopamine is. However, methamphetamine behaves differently. Methamphetamine slows down the normal breakdown of dopamine into an inactive substance. Therefore, dopamine accumulates in cells. Some of that excess then flows out of cells and alters the behavior of nearby neurons. That, in turn, causes methamphetamine's stimulatory effects on the brain.

Cell Receptors

A receptor is a protein on a cell, or sometimes inside a cell, to which a certain chemical attaches. Receptors receive cell signals. The signals come in the form of chemicals that attach to the receptors. Once attached, the chemical influences how the cell functions. Cells have many different kinds of receptors. Virtually all drugs attach to receptors.

Receptors are essential in controlling cellular activities. Every cell has many—perhaps even hundreds—of different receptor types. Each type has a specific, natural chemical that attaches to it. Drugs that bind to receptors send messages to a cell. Many drugs give excessive signals to cells simply because there is so much drug present. Psychoactive drugs, for example, often bind to brain neuron receptors and overstimulate the release of chemicals.

Drug Inactivation and Clearance

A drug does not stay in the body forever. Eventually its effects wear off as it breaks down into inactive forms and leaves the body. Cells in the liver and kidneys also play a role in ending a drug's effects as it passes through these organs.

The liver is the body's most effective detoxifying organ. Drug molecules in the bloodstream pass repeatedly through the liver. Its cells modify the chemical structure of many substances, including drugs. These altered chemical substances, called metabolites, are usually less active than the original drug. Thus, as the liver converts a drug into a metabolite, the drug's effects wear off.

The metabolites of some drugs, however, may temporarily produce a more powerful effect than the initial drug. For example, heroin is not itself an active drug. Instead, it is metabolized into morphine once inside the body.

While liver cells—and other tissues to some degree—are metabolizing a drug, the kidneys are at

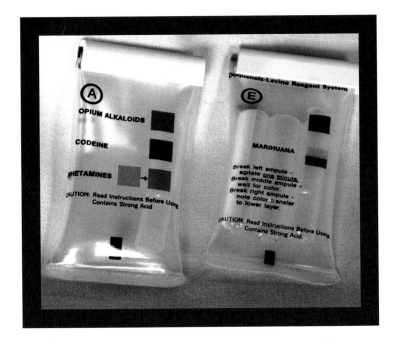

URINE TESTS DETECT DRUGS BECAUSE A DRUG'S TRACES, OR METABOLITES, APPEAR IN A PERSON'S URINE.

work, too. They remove drugs and metabolites from the blood. Drug substances that pass through the kidneys enter the urine formed there, then are excreted from the body.

Drugs that mix well with fats (lipids) tend to linger in the body longer than do water-soluble drugs. That is because the drugs settle into fat cells and into the layers of lipids that surround nerve cells. Most psychoactive drugs mix well with lipids. Some, such as the stimulant and hallucinogen PCP, may linger in a person's fatty tissues for days after effects on the brain have worn off.

A person's health or age influences how quickly a drug is metabolized. People who have liver or kidney disease, or children and elderly people, cannot metabolize or clear drugs as well as healthy adults do. In such vulnerable people, a drug's effects may be prolonged. Multiple doses, even when taken as directed, can add up to overdose levels because each dose lasts longer than it should. (Drug manufacturers assume a person has a healthy liver and kidneys when deciding a medicine's dosage.) A drug user's gender affects how a drug is metabolized. Generally, a woman's body breaks down drugs more slowly than a man's. Body size also matters. Alcohol or other drugs have stronger effects in a smaller person because a smaller body has less blood, fewer tissues, and smaller organs into which the drug disperses.

Drug Dependence
A key feature of illicit drugs, but also of some legal substances, such as alcohol, tobacco, and certain prescription drugs, is that they are habit-forming. If someone has been taking a drug for a period of time, he or she may find it difficult to quit.

Dependence in a drug user may occur when the body's normal biochemical activities have become so accustomed to the drug's presence that the absence of the drug causes withdrawal symptoms. Common withdrawal reactions may include nausea and vomiting, severe abdominal pain, profuse sweating, uncontrollable trembling, seizures, mental disorientation, hallucinations, and sometimes death.

Dependence may also occur when a drug user is unable to stop taking a substance even though he or she knows it is damaging in some way. Such dependence can disrupt a person's ability to carry out normal daily activities because of obsessive thinking about the drug.

Drugs That Cause Dependence
The most powerful dependency-generating drugs are opioids (heroin, morphine, fentanyl), cocaine, nicotine, alcohol, and amphetamines. They may cause dependence after only a few uses. Although it is not entirely clear yet why some drugs generate dependence more than others, it appears that they act more strongly on the brain's pleasure circuit. This reward circuit is a group of interconnected neurons from several regions of the brain that create and manage sensations of pleasure.

Some people appear to be genetically predisposed to becoming dependent to highly addictive drugs such as opioids, though everyone is susceptible. In the case of morphine and related pain-soothing opioid drugs, doctors assure patients that these drugs will not usually cause dependence if taken as prescribed. Opioids are extremely important for helping people who are injured, recovering from surgery, or have cancer or other illnesses with unremitting pain. If dependence does develop, a

16

gradual dose reduction will help the patient get off the drug with minimal withdrawal symptoms. But some people struggle with dependence to opioids long after the painful condition has healed.

Benzodiazepines, which are drugs prescribed to treat insomnia and anxiety, do not usually cause dependency if taken as directed. Some doctors and citizens' health groups warn, however, that many people have developed dependency to benzo-diazepines.

Several studies indicate that some marijuana users show signs of psychological dependence and withdrawal. Symptoms are milder than those generated by opiates, nicotine, or alcohol.

Certain other drugs, while physically harmful, are less likely to cause dependence. In general, hallucinogens, such as LSD and mescaline, and inhalants, such as gasoline and glues, do not appear to cause dependence readily. Antidepressants cause withdrawal symptoms in some people, suggesting a level of dependence. But these drugs do not cause cravings and obsessive drug-seeking behavior to the degree that heroin and cocaine do.

Caffeine creates a mild dependence in many people. They may experience headaches, mood swings, daytime sleepiness and fatigue, and inability to concentrate when they stop taking caffeine.

Over-the-counter drugs, which are sold without a doctor's prescription, are not supposed to create dependency. These common medications have met

Pleasure Circuit

Neurobiologists, scientists who study the brain, have found certain areas of the brain that are involved in both pleasure and drug dependence. Nerve cells in those areas connect with others by way of long, narrow extensions called axons, which release neurotransmitters—chemicals that attach to and influence adjacent cells. These neurons and axonal pathways are called the pleasure circuit, or reward circuit. Neurons in the pleasure circuit connect information about enjoyable sensations—the taste and smell of food or feelings of sexual arousal, for example—with neurons elsewhere that store thoughts and memories of those activities. Those memories create a longing for that activity and seeking behavior—a desire to do it again. That desire prompts an individual to take steps to repeat the experience.

Experts view this pleasure circuit as an ancient arrangement of neurons that ensures the survival of the organism—and its species—particularly in connection with food and sex.

It is difficult to explain the sensation of pleasure. But it certainly has to do with brain chemicals that neurons release in the pleasure circuit. The neurotransmitter dopamine is one of those chemicals. In fact, a vital part of the pleasure circuit is the mesolimbic dopamine pathway in the middle of the brain. The pathway consists of dopamine-secreting neurons in an area called the ventral tegmental area (VTA) and their axonal extensions to

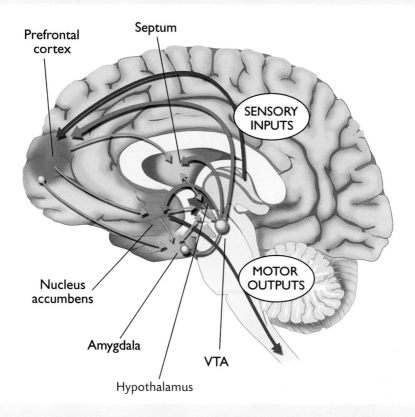

Prefrontal cortex
Septum
SENSORY INPUTS
Nucleus accumbens
MOTOR OUTPUTS
Amygdala
VTA
Hypothalamus

neurons in a nearby area, the nucleus accumbens. Neurons in the VTA receive signals about pleasurable sensations that originate outside the brain: sights, sounds, aromas, touch, and so on. Thoughts and reminders of the activity (as in seeing a picture of a favorite dessert, for example) also activate the same pathway. VTA neurons then release dopamine from their axon tips into the nucleus accumbens and other areas of the brain, as do the nucleus accumbens neurons. Thus, many cells are linked in a network tied to a pleasurable experience, such as drug-taking. Neurons in the hip-pocampus section of the brain appear to store memories of the experience, while those in the amygdala link emotions to it. Neurons in the cerebral cortex collect all the information related to a drug-taking experience and make necessary moment-to-moment decisions, such as where to go to take it and how much to use.

a requirement of the Food and Drug Administration (FDA) that they will not get people hooked when taken as directed. Yet some people report dependency problems with nasal decongestant sprays, pain medications—many of which contain caffeine with the painkiller—and sleep-enhancing antihistamines, such as those in nighttime cold remedies. Also, dextromethorphan (DXM) is an opioid in many cough medications that has become a drug of abuse. Taken in overdose—ten times or more the recommended dose—DXM may create dependence.

Tolerance
Many drugs produce a reaction known as tolerance, which occurs when a dose of the drug has reduced effects after repeated use over a period of days, weeks, or months. Tolerance happens because the drug chronically overstimulates cells, which then diminish their response to it. For example, a drug that mimics dopamine will cause a rush of pleasure, just as dopamine would. But with repeated drug exposure, the responding cells change. The number of receptors for that drug diminishes—a phenomenon called receptor down-regulation. With fewer receptors to which it can attach, the drug's effects are lessened. Because of tolerance, a drug user must take ever-increasing doses to flood the existing receptors in an attempt to feel the same sensations that lower doses used to give. Higher doses greatly increase the possibility of dependence. In fact, tolerance is a sign of drug dependence. Cocaine users

often say they never again achieve the intense euphoria experienced the first time, even if they subsequently consume larger and more frequent doses. Moreover, higher doses of a drug to which tolerance does *not* develop may cause damaging toxic effects.

Withdrawal

Withdrawal is a physical reaction to stopping a drug. Symptoms range from unpleasant to life threatening, depending on the drug and the extent of a person's prior usage. Withdrawal is an indicator that a person has become dependent on a drug. Symptoms occur because cells had readjusted their activities to create a new homeostasis—a new chemical balance—in the presence of the drug. Without the drug, normal homeostasis must be reestablished as the body goes from a pattern of functioning in a drug-influenced state to one of functioning without the drug. This helps explain why withdrawal symptoms often are the opposite of the drug's usual effects. For example, opiates such as heroin enhance the GABA neurotransmitter system. The general effect of the GABA system is to dampen brain activity and energy level. Withdrawal from opiates brings symptoms of heightened stimulation—intense hyperactivity, severe muscle aches and spasms, inability to sleep, and persistent penile erection. Digestive symptoms, such as severe abdominal cramps, vomiting, and diarrhea, indicate withdrawal reactions involving digestive tract cells. These cells also have opioid receptors, which likely had become dependent on the drug.

Drug Interactions
Drugs have the potential to cause serious reactions when taken in combination, even if each one alone would be safe. For example, the combination of alcohol with sleeping pills (benzodiazepines, barbiturates) or with a drug called GHB, has killed people because they are all depressants. Together they can push heart rate and breathing too low to sustain life.

Combinations of depressants and stimulants can have unpredictable, potentially dangerous effects. Cocaine taken with alcohol also can be deadly. Heroin and cocaine combined can be fatal.

Hundreds—perhaps thousands—of potentially harmful drug effects may occur when drug takers combine prescription and over-the-counter medications. Anyone who is already taking a drug, or even a nutritional supplement or naturopathic remedy, should always consult a doctor or pharmacist before adding another drug to the mix.

Side Effects
Side effects happen because a drug interacts with a complex chemical system: the human body. These effects, which are often undesirable, are unrelated to the drug's purpose. Drugs that dry up a runny nose can make a person sleepy, for example. Problematic side effects are called adverse effects or

adverse events. They may range from mild and annoying, to disruptive, to possibly deadly. Prescription drugs typically have the most serious and numerous side effects. (That is one of the reasons they are sold by prescription and not over the counter.) Examples of minor side effects are headaches, nausea, skin itching, cough, or dizziness. Less common, but far worse, are kidney or liver damage, heart attack, seizures, and other injuries involving vital organs. The most common side effects discovered during a drug's testing phase are written on the packaging of prescription drugs and in books such as the *Physician's Desk Reference* (PDR), or can be found on the Internet.

Drug Allergy

Some people are allergic to a drug (or to colorings, flavorings, artificial sweeteners, or other non-drug substances combined with it). An allergic reaction may not show up with the first use of a drug but at a second or subsequent exposure to the same drug or a closely related one. Allergies develop because a person's immune system overreacts to the "foreign" chemical in the drug. This triggers an inflammatory reaction, which is the body's response to injury or irritation. Many cells and chemicals are involved. Inflammation shows up as red, swollen, tender areas when fluid and cells from the bloodstream collect at the injury site. (Inflammation of internal organs cannot be seen but often is painful.) Some allergies

Drugs and Homeostasis: Shifting the Balance

In a healthy body, cellular activities are constantly working to maintain a state of balance on many levels: within individual cells, within tissues and organs, and within the body as a whole. That state of balance, homeostasis, ensures good health, while also allowing for adaptation to the needs of any moment. The brain, for example, receives a variety of internal and external cues that determine whether it should be in an alert state, a sleeping (unconscious) state, or somewhere in between. Other variables that are kept in balance through homeostasis, with flexibility to shift in one direction or another as needed, include nutrient levels, hormone concentrations, muscle tension, red blood cell number, and much more. Homeostasis relies on naturally produced chemicals to adjust cellular activities. Many drugs temporarily disrupt these chemicals. Stimulant drugs, for example, increase the amounts of neurotransmitters in the brain that keep neurons active and the person alert and energized, overriding signals to the brain that say "it's time to rest."

show up merely as an itchy skin rash. But other reactions can include rapid swelling of inflamed airways so that breathing is difficult, or anaphylactic shock—a sudden drop in blood volume as fluid leaks out of capillaries everywhere as part of a widespread inflammation. Emergency medical treatment is needed to rescue someone from these more severe kinds of allergic reactions.

If someone is aware of an allergy to a substance, she or he must carefully read the ingredients of over-the-counter products and tell a doctor or pharmacist before taking any prescribed medication. People with life-threatening drug reactions should always carry a note in their wallets or purses, or wear a Medic Alert bracelet with drug allergy information. This will provide caregivers with important information during a medical emergency (whether related to the allergy or not) if the individual becomes unconscious or cannot speak.

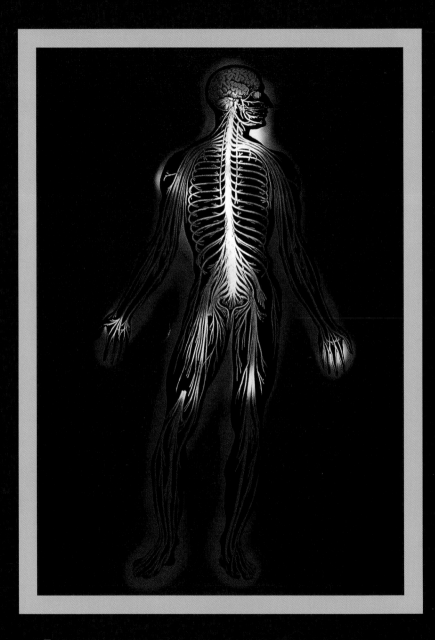

THE NERVOUS SYSTEM IS AN IMPORTANT SITE OF ACTION FOR MANY ILLICIT DRUGS. THE MOST POPULAR LEGALIZED DRUGS—ALCOHOL, NICOTINE, AND CAFFEINE—ACT THERE.

2 DRUGS AND THE NERVOUS SYSTEM

The central nervous system is often compared to a computer, but it is vastly more complex. It carries out thousands of tasks simultaneously. It controls the body's life-sustaining activities. It allows a person to use muscles. The brain, in particular, is the central processor of information and the decision maker. It makes sense out of sounds, sights, smells, and other external information. It integrates that information with memories, emotions, thoughts, and more. The brain decides what a person should do in response to situations. It generates desires for such things as food, water, companionship, sex—and sometimes drugs.

The nervous system uses chemicals to carry out all these tasks. Drugs can interfere with the chemical activities in the brain. While medications interfere in ways that may benefit a person, many illicit drugs derail normal brain activities and get a person hooked.

A drug that influences the nervous system may disrupt its network of interconnected neurons. Alcohol, for example, can make a person behave more boldly due to its effects on judgment. It also impairs muscle coordination (under the control of motor neurons) and dampens a person's awareness of surroundings (as perceived by sensory neurons). Because the brain is so complex, neurobiologists only partly understand its workings. One simplified way they describe the brain is in three parts, which are associated with three different types of functions.

The first and most basic part is the brainstem, also called the medulla oblongata. It is the area adjacent to the spinal cord. It controls the body's life-support systems, such as the rate and depth of breathing and the rate and strength of heart contractions. Those activities do not require conscious thought (though they can be influenced by emotions and conscious thoughts). The brainstem also controls certain automatic reflexes such as sneezing, coughing, swallowing, and vomiting.

Drugs, such as stimulants and depressants, influence the brainstem's control of life-support systems. Some over-the-counter medications influence the brainstem as well. Cold and allergy medications, for example, have ingredients that lessen

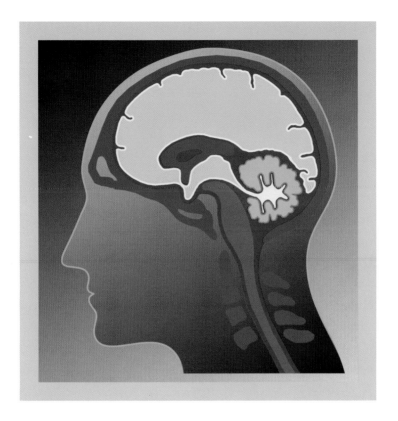

DRUGS THAT CROSS THE BLOOD-BRAIN BARRIER MAY NEGATIVELY AFFECT CELLS IN ALL THREE MAJOR AREAS OF THE BRAIN: THE BRAINSTEM, LIMBIC SYSTEM, AND CEREBRAL CORTEX.

the urge to cough or sneeze. Prescription medications and certain drugs used in the emergency room, such as those that reduce nausea and vomiting or that improve heart function, influence brainstem activities in beneficial ways.

The second part of the brain is the limbic system. It consists of several interconnected groups of neurons within the brain. This system generates emotions and mood, linking them to memories, thoughts, behaviors, and sensory information. Several prescription medications influence the limbic system beneficially. Antidepressants, which are drugs that treat psychological depression, are an example. However, some illicit drugs that cause dependence may impact the limbic system negatively.

The third part of the brain is the cerebral cortex. This large area creates and stores thoughts, reasoning, memory, creativity, language, and learned information. The cerebral cortex also initiates voluntary, or intentional, muscle movements. It can trigger muscular reflexes that are normally controlled by the brainstem, such as when a person chooses to cough. Both illicit drugs and prescription drugs have some impact on the cerebral cortex.

The three parts—brainstem, limbic system, and cerebral cortex—form a highly coordinated system. A simple example of how they work together is when someone with allergies inhales plant pollen in the air. The pollen triggers a sneeze, controlled by the brainstem. That might arouse feelings of annoyance, which take place in the limbic system. Finally, the cortex gets involved with thoughts ("It must be pollen season again.") and perhaps memories ("This happened the last time I walked in the woods."). The cortex also generates reasoned responses, such as getting out a tissue immediately and planning to buy an allergy medication in the future.

Nicotine provides an example of a drug that can interact with all three functional parts of the brain. It makes the heart beat faster and blood vessels in the skin narrow—actions carried out by the brainstem. Nicotine also creates a sensation of energy and pleasure within the limbic system. Finally, nicotine (and smoking in general) triggers responses in the cortex. For example, a smoker may think, "I feel calmer now that I have something to do with my hands," or "I know this isn't good for me, so maybe I'll quit—tomorrow."

Neurotransmitter Systems
Neurons in different regions of the brain communicate with one another via axons. At the ends of those extensions, neurons release chemical neurotransmitters, which influence the activities of nearby cells in this way:

> **1** A stimulus, such as a chemical, activates a neuron.
>
> **2** The activated neuron releases its own chemical, or neurotransmitter, from the end of an axon.
>
> **3** The neurotransmitter attaches momentarily to a protein receptor on a nearby cell, which triggers a response in that cell.
>
> **4** The neurotransmitter then leaves the receptor and is either destroyed or taken back into the neuron that released it.

Each neuron produces only one kind of neurotransmitter. However, many kinds of neurons, and many kinds of neurotransmitters, work in the nervous system. Neurobiologists are discovering new ones all the time.

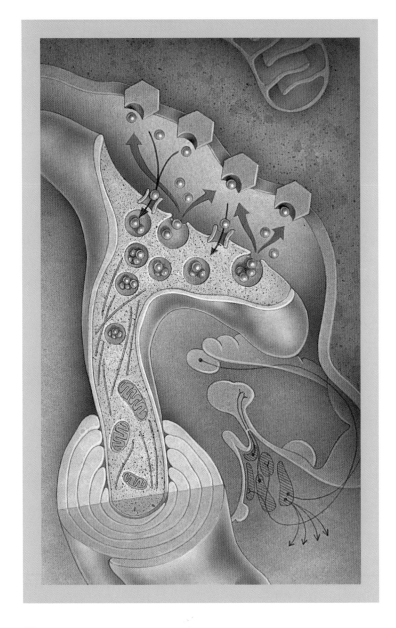

MANY DRUGS ACTIVATE NEURONS THAT RELEASE THE NEUROTRANSMITTER DOPAMINE, WHICH LOCKS ONTO CELL RECEPTORS TEMPORARILY. ONCE THE CELL RESPONDS, THE ORIGINAL NEURON EITHER REUSES THE DOPAMINE OR DESTROYS IT.

Psychoactive Drugs

Most illegal drugs are psychoactive and influence mental processes. They may also change a variety of other bodily functions that the brain controls, such as muscle coordination or heart rate. For instance, a person who has consumed too much alcohol may have trouble walking. Someone who has taken caffeine pills to stay awake may have a racing heartbeat.

Psychoactive drugs interfere with one or several neurotransmitter systems, often because the drugs' molecular structures resemble a neurotransmitter's structure. Various psychoactive drugs influence the neurotransmitters dopamine, serotonin, norepinephrine, GABA (gamma-aminobutyric acid), and acetylcholine (ACh). Marijuana acts on the endocannabinoid system. Heroin and related drugs influence the endogenous opioid system. (Researchers discovered both of those systems while studying how the drugs influence the brain.)

Drugs of abuse—those that create pleasurable sensations as well as dependency—all appear to increase the activity of the brain's dopamine neurotransmitter system. Drugs that produce a surge of dopamine among neurons in the pleasure circuit create a heightened sense of joy or energy. Users of such pleasure-inducing drugs describe the feeling as ecstasy, elation, euphoria, a "high" or "rush," and so on. As the drug is cleared from the body and dopamine levels in the brain fall, the drug user "crashes" and must endure a lower state of happiness or energy than normal. The crash phase often motivates a drug user to seek another dose.

Other neurotransmitters besides dopamine contribute to a sense of well-being. Natural, endogenous opioids—the endorphins, especially—are an example. Serotonin, epinephrine, and others also participate in creating these feelings. Drugs that increase the amounts of these neurotransmitters elevate mood and can become drugs of abuse as dependency on them sets in.

Stimulants

Several illicit drugs, and some widely used legal ones, stimulate the central nervous system. Stimulants "rev up" mental and physical processes. They increase alertness, energy level, physical stamina, and a sense of well-being, while diminishing appetite.

The part of the nervous system that responds to a stimulant's boost of alertness and energy is called the sympathetic nervous system. Signals carried by this part of the nervous system rev up the body, increasing its energy usage, muscle activity, and physical stamina. The sympathetic nervous system is always active to some degree but is balanced by the opposing actions of the parasympathetic nervous system. This system is another network of nerves that calm and slow the body's processes. Together, the sympathetic and parasympathetic systems reach a balance in their control of the body's many activities. But a drug can push the balance one way or the other, creating excess activity (as stimulants do) or excess relaxation (as depressants do).

Some stimulants directly activate the dopamine neurotransmitter system. This contributes to a drug's sensations of pleasure and also to the user's desire to take it again. Many stimulants activate serotonin and norepinephrine neurotransmitter systems. This is not so surprising since dopamine, serotonin, and norepinephrine all have very similar molecular structures. The norepinephrine system probably contributes most to the burst of energy a stimulant provides.

The most popular stimulants on the illegal drug market are amphetamines—methamphetamine and MDMA, or Ecstasy—and cocaine. Methylphenidate (Ritalin) is a stimulant, too. It is prescribed for attention deficit hyperactivity disorder (ADHD). However, Ritalin has become a drug of abuse as well.

Two popular legal drugs are stimulants: caffeine (in coffee, sodas, teas, energy drinks, some foods, and pills) and nicotine (in cigarettes, cigars, chewing tobacco, and smoking cessation products, such as nicotine patches and gums).

Amphetamines
Amphetamine stimulants share a molecular structure with the neurotransmitters dopamine, norepinephrine, and serotonin. Neurons mistake amphetamine molecules for these important brain neurotransmitters. However, these drugs do have some different properties than the body's natural versions. For example, neurons that make dopamine take it back

into the cell shortly after releasing it. Certain proteins on the neurons' surfaces, called dopamine transporters, escort the dopamine back inside. However, illegal drugs that mimic dopamine, such as methamphetamine, may permanently damage the endings of dopamine-producing cells, affecting normal dopamine production.

Cocaine

Like amphetamines, cocaine is a stimulant that strengthens the influence of the neurotransmitters dopamine, norepinephrine, and serotonin. Cocaine molecules interact with dopamine transporter proteins, as amphetamines do, but in slightly different ways. Overall, the effects are similar: an increase in dopamine in the brain, which enhances sensations of pleasure.

Cocaine does this by binding to dopamine transporter proteins and blocking them from being carried back into neurons. As dopamine accumulates outside of neurons, it stimulates nearby cells excessively, including those in the pleasure circuit. Cocaine also increases the amounts of active norepinephrine and serotonin in the brain, contributing to the drug's effects. Since cocaine does not increase the amount of dopamine *inside* a neuron, it does not appear to damage dopamine-producing cells at high doses, as methamphetamine does. However, cocaine is known to cause serious mental disturbances when taken in high, binge-level doses.

Ritalin

Ritalin is a prescription stimulant that is prescribed to "settle down" people with attention deficit hyperactivity disorder—ADHD. Since stimulant drugs can make a person without ADHD agitated, anxious, and unable to concentrate, experts are not sure how Ritalin helps a person with ADHD calm down and concentrate on tasks. One thought is that people with ADHD have *lower* dopamine levels than normal and that these lower levels somehow cause their symptoms. Ritalin supposedly brings their dopamine levels closer to normal.

Ritalin's actions are quite similar to cocaine's. The Ritalin molecule attaches to dopamine transporter proteins and prevents dopamine-releasing neurons from transporting dopamine back inside. Dopamine levels rise in the brain, activating responsive neurons.

While Ritalin is able to help many people function better, it is becoming a drug of abuse by people who do not need it. Though it is illegal to use a drug that was prescribed for someone else, some people abuse Ritalin for its stimulant effects: wakefulness, appetite suppression, and euphoria. Abusers take the tablets orally or crush them and snort the powder, or even dissolve them in water and inject the mixture—all potentially dangerous.

Nicotine

A component of tobacco, nicotine is a common, legal stimulant. Nicotine has been described as one of the most rapidly and strongly addictive substances. Tobacco is usually smoked, though some people chew it. People trying to break a nicotine addiction take small doses in gum, nasal spray, or skin patches.

Nicotine acts on the nervous system by influencing the acetylcholine (ACh) neurotransmitter system. Nicotine attaches to certain receptors (called nicotinic receptors) to which ACh normally binds. Those receptors are present on cells in many areas of the brain. When ACh or nicotine binds, the receptors interact with proteins in the cell's membrane that allow sodium and calcium ions to flow into the cell. The flow of ions triggers a response by the cell. Cells in the brain's pleasure circuit have ACh receptors, which release dopamine and produce the pleasurable sensations typical of a stimulant.

Experts believe one or more substances besides nicotine make tobacco smoking addictive and are researching their chemical nature. These substances can act to increase dopamine, too, but in a different way than nicotine does.

Caffeine

The most popular drug in the world is caffeine. It is a stimulant, consumed as a beverage from naturally occurring plant sources—coffee, tea, maté, guarana—and in soft drinks or energy drinks (to which it is added), as well as in some foods, such as coffee-flavored ice cream. It is also naturally present in chocolate in small amounts.

Caffeine and two similar molecules, theophylline and theobromine, are stimulants found in certain plants and belong to a chemical group called the methylxanthines. These chemicals act as central nervous system stimulants indirectly, by preventing the natural sleep-inducing chemical, adenosine, from attaching to brain neurons. By blocking adenosine's actions, methylxanthines keep the brain from going into a resting phase.

People who use caffeine experience enhanced alertness, increased attention for performing mental tasks, and increased feelings of energy and well-being. Caffeine has been shown to improve sports performance. But too much caffeine can cause the "jitters"—shakiness, nervousness, and poor concentration.

Depressants

Depressant drugs, both legal and illegal, are a diverse group. Terms for these drugs include sedatives, sleeping pills, antianxiety medications, tranquilizers, hypnotics, soporifics, and downers (a street term). Alcohol is also a depressant. So are "date rape" drugs such as GHB and Rohypnol, which cause a rape victim to become groggy and weak.

Normally, the brain uses information from the environment and from activities within the body to create an appropriate level of wakefulness or sleepiness at each moment. However, depressants interfere with that. They induce calm, relaxation, and sleepiness through their actions on brain neurotransmitter systems. Depressants may also cause disorientation, altered perceptions, confusion, and poor memory. They can alter judgment, emotions, and behavior.

In addition, depressants modify functions outside the brain that are under its control, such as voluntary muscle movement (including tongue and lip muscles used in speech). The result may be clumsiness, muscle weakness, and slurred speech. Because of these combined effects, depressants can turn normally safe activities, such as driving or operating machinery, into dangerous ones.

Alcohol and prescription benzodiazepines are the most common depressants. However, other kinds of drugs, such as opiates, antihistamines in allergy and cold/flu medications, and motion-sickness medications, can cause drowsiness, too. Depressants in overdose or in combinations (alcohol together with sleeping pills, for instance) have killed many people. This happens because high doses or drug combinations create too deep a state of relaxation. Under these conditions, the brainstem region responds by slowing its signals to the heart and the muscles involved in breathing. Blood flow and oxygen then plummet to levels that cannot sustain life.

> **Depressants' Actions on the Nervous System**
>
> Many depressants influence the GABA (gamma-aminobutyric acid) neurotransmitter system in this way:
>
> 1 Depressant drugs interact with protein on cells that respond to GABA .
>
> 2 The attached drug forces a change in the shape of the nearby GABA receptor.
>
> 4 These receptors are now *better* at holding on to GABA.
>
> 5 GABA stays attached longer and thus inhibits neuronal activities more than usual.

Alcohol

Alcohol interferes with GABA as do other depressants. Evidence from scientific studies shows that it affects several other neurotransmitter systems, including glutamate, acetylcholine (ACh), and serotonin. Alcohol probably has widespread influence because it is a small molecule, which resembles some portion of each of these neurotransmitters.

Benzodiazepines

Benzodiazepines (such as Xanax, Valium, Klonopin, Ativan) are among the most widely prescribed of all drugs. Doctors recommend them to patients who need help sleeping or who are worried or anxious enough that these feelings disrupt normal daily

41

activities. Doctors also prescribe benzodiazepines to ease alcohol withdrawal symptoms, help a patient relax before surgery, or control epilepsy seizures. Benzodiazepines rarely cause death due to overdose (unless combined with alcohol or other depressants). However, people may become dependent on them and have withdrawal symptoms when they try to stop.

The Breathalyzer Test

Alcohol is released in small amounts from the lungs as vapor in proportion to the amount in the bloodstream. "Breathalyzer" tests given to drivers suspected of driving while intoxicated make use of that. Exhaled air from the suspect is collected and its alcohol content measured, typically by a series of chemical reactions that can be done on the spot. And though a person may attempt to mask the aroma of alcohol with breath mints, that has no influence on Breathalyzer readings.

"Date Rape" Drugs

Depressants can sedate a person to such a degree that he or she is unable to walk or stand and is unaware of what is happening. These reactions make a person vulnerable to abuse. This is why some depressants are being used as "date rape" drugs. An abuser may secretly add this kind of depressant to the beverages of a victim, then abuse that person sexually. The victim lacks the ability to fight back or even to recall later what happened.

42

The most common date rape drugs are GHB (gamma-hydroxybutyric acid), Rohypnol (a benzo-diazepine now banned from the U.S. market), and ketamine (an anesthetic commonly used by veteri-narians). Two other benzodiazepines similar to Rohypnol, Xanax and Klonopin, are also becoming significant drugs of abuse. Besides muscle weakness and mental confusion, the drugs can also cause dizziness, breathing difficulty, amnesia, and coma (an extended period of unconsciousness). They can kill, too, by shutting down the brain's signals that keep a person breathing.

Ketamine, which is added to beverages, smoked with tobacco or marijuana, or injected, has been described as producing an out-of-body sensation. How it does so is not yet clear. It does not seem to influence GABA as many depressants do, but may block the brain's stimulatory neurotransmitter sys-tems. GHB and Rohypnol act by increasing the activity of the GABA neurotransmitter system; GHB, at least, appears to influence several other brain chemicals. GHB once was a popular body-building substance (it increases growth hormones, which enlarge muscles) but proved to cause dependency. It is now a controlled substance.

Antidepressants

Antidepressants are prescription drugs that influ-ence a person's mood and are prescribed to treat clinical depression. Antidepressants share some fea-tures of stimulant drugs. The most commonly prescribed antidepressant medications increase the amount of one or several of the monoamine neuro-transmitters in the brain: dopamine, norepineph-rine, and serotonin. Those neurotransmitters each have some role in pleasurable emotions, such as joy, satisfaction, and elation.

Antidepressants' Actions on the Nervous System

Two popular kinds of antidepressant drugs are the MAOIs and the SSRIs. MAOIs stands for monoamine oxidase inhibitors. SSRIs stands for selective seratonin reuptake inhibitors, which are newer than the MAOIs.

1 MAOIs block the action of the enzyme monoamine oxidase, which breaks down the neurotransmitters dopamine, norepinephrine, and serotonin. MAOIs allow those neurotrans-mitters to accumulate, improving mood.

2 SSRIs act only on serotonin, preventing it from being taken immediately back into neurons that release it. Serotonin therefore is available to bind repeatedly to neurons that respond by generating feelings of well-being.

The SSRI antidepressant drugs, such as Prozac and Zoloft, are among the most frequently pre-scribed drugs. They boost serotonin's actions in the brain. Serotonin levels are measurably lower in the bloodstream of depressed people (which indicates lower amounts in their brains). Serotonin partici-pates in many kinds of brain activity. Low amounts are also found in people who suffer from certain food cravings, eating disorders, premenstrual mood changes, and seasonal affective disorder (depression related to reduced sunlight as days shorten in the fall). SSRIs can improve these conditions.

The SSRIs have come under scrutiny, however. Some people who are taking them, especially teenagers, have unexpectedly become violent. A few have committed suicide while taking these drugs. While researchers try to clarify whether this is a side effect of the drug or is related more to a person's history and severity of his or her depression, warnings are included with these drugs to alert people to these dangers.

Opiates

The opiate drugs include morphine, heroin, codeine, and fentanyl—all effective pain relievers. Opiates have some depressant effects, causing relaxation, sleepiness, and lack of awareness of surroundings, as well as reduced breathing. Opiates act as depressants in complex ways involving several neurotransmitter systems in the brain and the spinal cord. Opiates influence the body's endogenous opioid system. When used carefully, opiates are indispensable in medical treatment. They allow a patient not just relief from pain, but deep rest, which enhances healing.

Heroin, once used medically, was recognized by the early 1900s as dangerous because it created strong dependency quickly. Now morphine is used medically, although it often results in a compulsion to use the drug.

Codeine, which is very similar chemically to morphine, is present in many over-the-counter cold and flu remedies. However, the doses are too small to elicit dependence when used as directed. Nonetheless, desperate drug abusers sometimes try to satisfy their cravings for opiates by taking over-the-counter drugs that contain codeine.

Opiates' Actions on the Nervous System

The opiate drugs mimic some activities of naturally occurring chemicals called endogenous opioids in this way:

1 Opiates bind to receptors for endogenous opioids on some of the neurons that produce the neurotransmitter GABA.

2 The drugs block release of GABA by the neurons.

3 When GABA release is blocked, dopamine-producing neurons are free to release more dopamine than usual.

4 One of the effects of excess dopamine in specific brain areas is dulling one's conscious awareness of pain.

Hallucinogens and Dissociative Drugs
Hallucinogens or dissociatives (also called psychotomimetic or psychedelic drugs) alter one's perception of reality. They have the ability to create

dreamlike images—both delightful and horrific—often with vivid colors, distortions of sound and sights, inaccurate perception of time, and so on.

These drugs appear to stimulate patterns of brain activity that usually occur during dreaming. As in dreaming, the drug user experiences visions, thoughts, sensations, and feelings unrelated to real objects and events at that moment. Hallucinogens can also induce strong emotional swings and impair reasoning.

Two main groups of hallucinogens resemble brain neurotransmitters. The tryptamine drugs, such as LSD and psilocybin, resemble the neurotransmitter serotonin. This chemical carries signals among neurons in areas of the brain involved in sensory perception, behavior, mood, hunger, sexual behavior, and more.

The phenethylamine drugs, such as mescaline, nexus (2-CB), and Ecstasy (MDMA, with stimulant properties, too) resemble the neurotransmitters dopamine and norepinephrine. Those neurotransmitters are widespread in many areas of the brain.

Dissociative drugs such as PCP (phencyclidine, "angel dust") and ketamine create sensations of detachment from reality, of being "out of body." Researchers first developed dissociative drugs as anesthetics, but some have become drugs of abuse. Like hallucinogens, dissociative drugs distort perceptions and can cause severe disorientation.

47

> **Hallucinogens' and Dissociatives' Action on the Nervous System**
>
> 1 Dissociative drugs, such as PCP and ketamine, appear to impact the glutamate neuro-transmitter system.
>
> 2 Specifically, the drugs block glutamate receptors (also called NMDA receptors). Glutamate is a key stimulatory neurotransmitter, which activates networks of neurons in many brain regions (including neurons of the dopamine and norepinephrine systems).

Marijuana

Marijuana produces some effects of depressants, stimulants, and hallucinogens. Many people who use marijuana report a sense of calm, relaxation, sleepiness, and euphoria, as well as an increase in appetite. The chemical delta-9-tetrahydrocannabinol (THC) is currently thought to be marijuana's primary psychoactive ingredient. Marijuana and purified THC influence the brain in many ways. They temporarily impair memory formation and clear thinking and can produce visual distortions, dizziness, and even anxiety, panic, or psychotic reactions in rare cases. Marijuana and THC-like chemicals also alleviate nausea and reduce awareness of pain. These properties have led to the development of THC-based drugs in the United States and Europe to help people tolerate cancer treatments and AIDS symptoms (nausea, pain, life-threatening weight loss).

THC attaches to cannabinoid receptors (so called for *Cannabis,* the marijuana plant's botanical name). The body has at least two types of those receptors. Some are present on neurons in several brain regions and others on cells outside the brain, especially in the digestive tract. Neurobiologists are still working out just how THC and the body's endogenous cannabinoids alter the activities of neurons.

Inhalants

Inhalants are substances of abuse that users breathe into the lungs until they experience mood- and perception-altering effects. Common examples are solvents (liquids that readily evaporate), which are present in glues, paints, paint removers, and felt-tip markers. Some people intentionally inhale fumes from fuels, such as gasoline and butane (in cigarette lighters), for the "high." In addition, gases that serve as anesthetics in medical or dental procedures are abused, especially nitrous oxide ("laughing gas").

Inhalants generally depress brain function and have effects similar to alcohol. However, their action is faster than alcohol, causing effects within seconds. These effects include drowsiness, slurred speech, light-headedness or dizziness, muscle weakness and poor coordination, euphoria, and sometimes hallucinations and delusions.

The inhalants are a diverse group chemically. Their actions on neurons vary. Toluene is a chemical in many inhalants that activates the brain's dopamine neurotransmitter system, probably contributing to dependence. Toluene also is toxic and destructive to many tissues. Over time it permanently damages the brain and nerves. The destructive effects may lead to neurological syndromes—collections of several nerve-related problems such as impaired vision, hearing, and muscle coordination, as well as mental impairment that can be severe. Inhalants also are toxic to other vital organs with repeated use. Just a single session of prolonged inhalant use can cause convulsions and seizures due to erratic brain activity, as well as coma and sudden death.

Anabolic Steroids

Steroids taken to build muscle (anabolic steroids) are similar to androgens, a group of steroid hormones that the body produces naturally. Doctors sometimes prescribe anabolic steroids to treat abnormally delayed growth or underdevelopment of reproductive features in young men. However, bodybuilders and some athletes use anabolic steroids to increase muscle mass and strength. When taken for nonmedical reasons (more frequently and at higher doses), anabolic steroids disrupt a control mechanism that keeps steroid levels in the bloodstream within normal, healthy ranges.

Men who use anabolic steroids have reported psychological changes, such as extreme mood swings,

---

Steroids' Actions on the Nervous System

Both natural androgens and artificial anabolic steroids influence regions of the brain where behaviors are programmed, including sexual behavior, aggression, and mood. Here is how they work:

1 Steroids affect cells by attaching to receptors inside a cell's nucleus. A receptor-steroid complex alters how the cell uses its DNA.

2 Artificial steroids take many days or weeks to create a noticeable effect because they change the amounts and kinds of proteins a cell makes.

---

increased feelings of aggression, violence, and heightened sexual interest while using the drugs. Depression can also set in when drug use is stopped. While studies have shown these changes to be related to steroid use, some researchers are cautious about concluding that anabolic steroids cause these behavioral changes. Instead, they suggest that men who choose to use steroids already have tendencies to be aggressive and highly sexually active. (Studies with laboratory animals clearly show that anabolic steroids increase these traits, however.)

Steroids are well known to affect normal brain development in humans (both men and women) and influence behavior in adults. A likely mechanism for the way anabolic steroids affect behavioral changes is through the involvement of the GABA neurotransmitter system. Receptors for GABA are abundant in regions of the brain involved in sexual behaviors, and studies of steroids' influence on brain GABA levels support this idea.

Over-the-Counter Drugs

Many over-the-counter medications influence the central nervous system in beneficial ways. Aspirin and ibuprofen are common pain relievers and fever reducers. They belong to a group of drugs called NSAIDs—nonsteroidal anti-inflammatory drugs.

These drugs diminish the perception of pain by the brain when it receives signals from nociceptors (pain-perceiving nerves).

Just how these drugs diminish pain and reduce fever is not fully understood. However, it is well established that NSAIDs block a cell's production of prostaglandins—lipidlike molecules with various functions. For instance, prostaglandins are released by injured cells, and prostaglandins make nearby nociceptors even more sensitive to pain.

Medications for colds, flu, and allergies often contain NSAIDs and antihistamines, which reduce swelling. Others have the opioid pain reliever codeine in low dose. Codeine and most antihistamines are central nervous system depressants and can cause drowsiness. Labels on these products warn users against driving a vehicle or using power equipment until all signs of drowsiness are gone.

Do Drugs Cause Mental Illness?

A serious concern about taking psychoactive drugs is that they may cause permanent brain damage. For example, at high doses, PCP mimics many aspects of schizophrenia, a mental disorder in which a person has delusions, hallucinations, disorganized thoughts and speech, and other abnormal behaviors and perceptions. There are cases of people who took drugs and later developed mental illness. But in those cases it is difficult to sort out whether drugs contributed to the illness or whether the choice or need for drug-taking was a part of a mental disorder that had not yet been identified. Studies that pinpoint which brain chemicals are influenced by drugs and which brain chemicals are abnormal in mental disorders should help clarify the link between drugs and mental illness.

Stimulants are available over the counter, too. Concentrated caffeine is available as pills; caffeine is also added to many pain medicines because, for reasons not clearly understood, the drug combination improves pain relief.

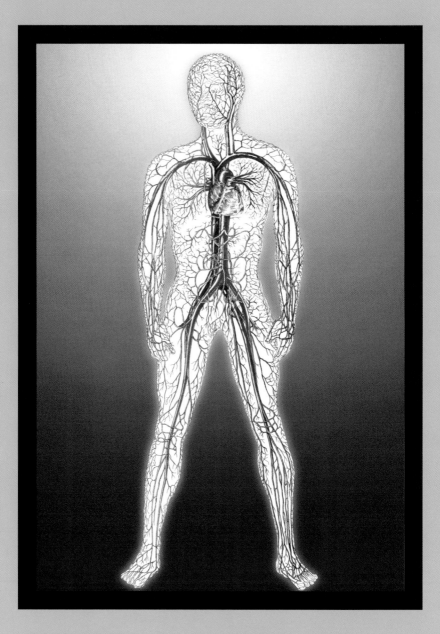

THE CARDIOVASCULAR SYSTEM IS VITAL TO THE ACTION OF MANY DRUGS.
IT CARRIES THEM FROM THEIR ROUTES OF ENTRY—MOUTH, NOSE, LUNGS,
INTESTINE, SKIN, OR INJECTED BLOOD VESSEL—THROUGHOUT THE BODY.

3 DRUGS AND THE CARDIOVASCULAR SYSTEM

The cardiovascular system is one of the human body's basic life-support systems. The heart (*cardio-*), blood vessels (*vascular*), and blood each play a part in the system's well-coordinated activities. The cardiovascular system can be likened to a network of highways and vehicles that go to all the body's "neighborhoods"—its groups of cells in every tissue and organ. Blood flows continually, delivering substances to cells, including drugs.

The heart keeps blood flowing by its contractions, which force blood into arteries. The speed and strength of the heart's contractions change according to the body's needs at any moment. The brain's cardiovascular center controls this process. The center's neurons either speed and stengthen or slow and relax the heart's pumping.

Nerves that strengthen and speed the heart's efforts are part of the sympathetic nervous system (described in Chapter 2). Nerves that slow it are part of the parasympathetic nervous system. Normally, these two sets of neurons are balanced to match the body's needs. But drugs can skew that balance.

Illegal drugs, and some over-the-counter products, interact with the cardiovascular system in a number of ways. For instance, stimulants increase signals that go out from the cardiovascular center to increase heart activity and mimic the sympathetic nervous system. On the other hand, depresants reduce signals going out from the cardiovascular center in the brain and mimic the parasympathetic nervous system.

Other drugs directly or indirectly influence the composition of blood. Aspirin, for example, is a pain relief drug that makes it harder for blood to clot, or thicken. Various illicit drugs, especially cocaine, make blood more likely to clot. Some athletes illegally use erythropoietin, a drug (and also a naturally occurring hormone), during the weeks prior to a competition. Erythropoietin stimulates the new red blood cells, which carry more oxygen and give an unfair advantage to these athletes.

Many prescription drugs are designed to slow or speed heart function, alter the lipid or fat content of blood, change blood vessel diameter, and so on. These drugs are among the most commonly prescribed medications to prevent or treat diseases of the heart or vasculature.

Route of Drug Entry

Nearly all drugs interact with the cardiovascular system. Injection of a drug into a vein is called intravenous delivery. A blood vessel that is easy to see and puncture—such as a vein in the arm, leg, or sometimes the torso—is used as the entry point for the injected drug. This direct entry route causes the strongest surge of drug influence because the cardiovascular system distributes the drug through the body in seconds. In a medical setting, intravenous delivery of a prescribed drug in safe doses, and administered in sterile conditions, can save someone's life.

On the other hand, injection of illicit drugs is riskier. Unless the skin is thoroughly cleaned beforehand, bacteria or other pathogens on the body's surface can gain direct entry into the bloodstream through the injection site. Sepsis, a bacterial infection of the bloodstream and of vital organs, is much more common in people who inject drugs than in people who do not. Sepsis can cause permanent organ damage. Even with medical care, sepsis is frequently fatal.

Injecting illegal drugs is associated with other problems, too. Sometimes people using illegal drugs share needles and syringes, transmitting deadly viral or bacterial pathogens to one other. Many drug users with hepatitis (liver infection) and HIV (human immunodeficiency virus) have spread their diseases by sharing needles. Furthermore, street drugs often are "laced" with other substances or harmful chemicals left over from making the drug. These impurities and toxins go directly into the bloodstream, where the cardiovascular system pumps them everywhere blood travels. Drug impurities can kill a person just as readily as overdoses can. When abused, even Ritalin, a prescription drug in pill form that treats ADHD (attention deficit hyperactivity disorder), can harm the cardiovascular system if the drug abuser dissolves the pills in water and injects the solution. A portion of the pill that does not fully dissolve may clog blood vessels, causing serious tissue damage.

Stimulants

Stimulants mimic the sympathetic nervous system's effects on the heart and blood vessels. They speed and strengthen the heart's contractions, and they narrow blood vessels somewhat. These changes can be mild and short-lived, as when someone consumes a lot of caffeine in a short time. Or the changes may be powerful and longer lasting, as in the case of drug abusers who take in high and repeated doses of amphetamines. Cocaine can even trigger fibrillation, an erratic heart rhythm in which heart contractions are rapid, uncoordinated, and unable to pump blood well. Fibrillation deprives organs of blood, including the brain. Within minutes of cocaine injection, a person can go into a coma, suffer permanent brain damage, or die.

Stimulants that raise blood pressure can cause serious problems. Blood pressure is the force with which blood flows through vessels. It is influenced by the heart's pumping power and the diameter of blood vessels. Normally, the cardiovascular center controls both of those in a healthy fashion. But drug stimulants interfere by mimicking the sympathetic nervous system and cause vessel-damaging high blood pressure. Blood vessels may rupture, especially if they are already damaged by arteriosclerosis, a condition marked by narrowed, inflexible blood vessels. Hemorrhagic stroke (loss of blood to the brain due to blood vessel rupture) is another serious potential result of high blood pressure. Stimulant drugs, especially cigarettes, increase a person's risk of arteriosclerosis and stroke.

Stimulants' Actions on the Cardiovascular System

1 Stimulants activate the brain's cardiovascular center.

2 Neurons to the heart signal the heart to accelerate pumping and heart contractions.

3 Other neuron signals from the cardiovascular center go to collections of small vessels, causing them to narrow.

4 With more blood pumping through narrowed blood vessels, blood pressure shoots up.

5 Stimulants may cause too-rapid or erratic signals to the heart, which may lead to ineffective heart rhythms and cardiovascular failure. Insufficient blood supply deprives brain cells of oxygen, causing coma, seizures, brain damage, or death.

Caffeine

Caffeine is the most widely used stimulant. Caffeine, whether in coffee, soda, tea, energy drinks, or pills, can increase heart rate and elevate blood pressure. The higher the dose, the stronger its cardiovascular effects. However, some people are especially sensitive to caffeine. They may react to very small amounts with a racing heartbeat and elevated blood pressure. These are not life threatening unless caffeine is consumed in massive overdose (hundreds of caffeine pills). Many studies, including some very large ones such as the Framingham Heart Study, have found no long-term cardiovascular harm.

Nicotine

Several cardiovascular health problems are associated with tobacco smoke. Nicotine, a stimulant, mimics the sympathetic nervous system's effects and increases heart activity and blood pressure. Also, smokers have higher cholesterol and lower levels of the beneficial substances HDLs in the bloodstream than nonsmokers do.

Nicotine, like many stimulants, boosts heart rate and narrows blood vessels, causing high blood pressure. Over time, recurrent high blood pressure damages arteries. They become diseased with arteriosclerosis, making them much more likely to become clogged and to deprive cells of blood supply. Blood clots, or blockages, form in the bloodstream of smokers more often than they do in the bloodstream of nonsmokers. Compounds from smoke appear to activate blood-borne proteins that help to form clots.

Nicotine alone appears not to underlie most long-term cardiovascular diseases related to smoking. Studies of people who use nicotine patches instead of smoking do not show increased risk of cardiovascular problems over nonsmokers. So it appears that other substances in smoke contribute to cardiovascular damage in smokers.

Nonsmokers who are in enclosed spaces with smokers inhale all the substances in tobacco smoke. It is estimated that 54,000 nonsmokers die each year in the United States from smoke-related cardiovascular disease.

Depressants

Depressant drugs—alcohol, opiates (heroin, morphine, fentanyl), GHB, benzodiazepines, barbiturates—diminish the heart's pumping ability by slowing and weakening heart contractions. Just how they do this isn't yet clear for every drug. However, depressants may decrease the brain's stimulatory neuron signals to the heart and to the blood vessels. Other depressants may act directly on heart muscle or vessels.

Young people who are new to alcohol's effects may unknowingly combine alcohol with other depressants while experimenting with drugs. Several deaths among college students in recent years due to alcohol overdose are a reminder that alcohol truly can kill. During a single session of depressant use, the greatest cardiovascular risk is that the brain may suffer anoxia—too little oxygen—because of sluggish blood flow. This may cause seizures, unconsciousness, coma, permanent brain damage, or death.

Prescription Drugs
Depressants—sedatives, sleeping pills, antianxiety medications—are intended to calm and relax a person. Benzodiazepines are the most commonly prescribed sedatives and sleeping aids. However, some drug users intentionally or accidentally take benzodiazepines while alcohol levels in their bloodstream are high. This has an additive depressant effect on the cardiovascular system. Such a combination has killed individuals even when the amount of each one alone would not have been fatal.

Alcohol
Alcohol depresses the brain's cardiovascular center, slowing heart rate and its pumping strength. Long-term excessive alcohol consumption damages cells of many organs, including heart muscle. Long-term excessive alcohol consumption is associated with arteriosclerosis and with related, often-fatal diseases: coronary heart disease, heart attack, and stroke. Scarring of the liver (cirrhosis) from alcohol abuse indirectly stresses the heart as it works

Depressants' Actions on the Cardiovascular System

1 Depressant drugs dampen the signals that the brain's cardiovascular center sends to the heart.

2 With fewer of these signals, heart rate slows and contractions weaken.

3 Depressants also diminish the sympathetic nervous system's effects on blood vessels, causing their dilation or expansion.

4 Blood pressure drops.

5 Flow of blood through the vasculature slows.

6 Oxygen delivery to the brain falls, impairing brain cell function.

harder to push blood through the damaged liver's vessels. An enlarged heart may result, but ultimately it fails to serve the body's demands for blood.

Marijuana

THC, marijuana's most well-studied ingredient, appears to interact directly with blood vessels. THC attaches to receptors on muscle cells that encircle blood vessels. Some researchers are exploring the details of how THC and the body's own similar chemicals, the endogenous cannabinoids, influence blood vessel diameter.

Receptor-bound THC appears to relax muscles around arteries, opening the vessels a bit more than usual. More blood flows into skin, brain, and other areas where arteries have relaxed. Blood pressure drops as arteries expand. Signals to the heart from the cardiovascular center of the brain may increase, speeding heart rate and contraction strength to compensate for the low pressure.

With long-term marijuana use, artery muscle cells may lower their receptor numbers as they become accustomed to overexposure. This may interfere with the body's own natural cannabinoids and their ability to control blood flow. In the brain, loss of normal control over blood flow in arteries might be related to long-term problems of marijuana use, such as memory loss, attention deficits, and learning problems.

Drug researchers have developed a pharmaceutical counterpart, or analog, of THC because it has some positive effects. THC's ability to relax arteries may help people in the throes of a heart attack. Experiments with animals have shown that THC and similar drugs keep blood flowing well and may prevent some of the heart muscle damage. Patients taking THC while undergoing chemotherapy may receive some relief from vomiting and nausea. Patients who experienced such relief were better able to maintain weight during chemotherapy than cancer patients not taking marijuana. While the U.S. Supreme Court in 2005 voted 6 to 3 that marijuana remain an illegal substance, synthetic THC is available by prescription for medicinal uses.

Inhalants

Inhalants are a diverse group of chemicals that impact the central nervous system and, indirectly, the cardiovascular system. Some are thought to influence the brain's cardiovascular center. Others are likely to act directly on heart muscle and blood vessels. Some inhalants, such as ether and nitrous oxide (anesthetics) and solvents and cleaners (toluene, benzene, and other vapors) depress the cardiovascular system. Combining such drugs with alcohol can kill users.

A disturbing trend among inhalant users is "sudden sniffing death syndrome." The user dies suddenly during inhalant use, especially of fuel fumes, because of heart failure. Sudden sniffing death syndrome causes at least half the deaths among inhalant users, including those using them for the first time. This type of inhalant use appears to stimulate the cardiovascular system. Heart activity can race out of control if the drug combines with other stimulations of the sympathetic nervous system, such as strenuous physical activity or even being startled or frightened. The overstimulated heart races and beats erratically, failing as a pump. Cause of death is insufficient blood delivery to the brain, just as in other types of heart attack.

Inhalants vary in their damaging effects. Anesthetic inhalants reduce activity of the brain's cardiovascular center. This, in turn, slows heart rate

INHALANT DRUGS HAVE MANY DIFFERENT CHEMICAL STRUCTURES, WITH DIFFERING DAMAGING WAYS OF ACTING ON THE HEART AND BLOOD VESSELS.

and pumping strength, and lowers blood pressure. Solvents and cleaners such as toluene, benzene, and methanol also are depressants. Nitrites cause a drop in blood pressure when they relax muscle around arteries. Blood flow slows. Skin feels warm as blood lingers in its vessels. The heart may beat more quickly and powerfully in an attempt to bring blood pressure up to normal.

Over-the-Counter Drugs
Few drugs that are readily available to the general public have strong effects on the cardiovascular system, but indirectly or in combination they can. Thousands of people take aspirin to protect against heart attack since it has the ability to hinder the formation of blood clots where they don't belong—in the bloodstream. Taking aspirin reduces the chances of fatal stroke, respiratory failure, or heart failure. The downside of taking aspirin is that it also can cause bleeding in the digestive tract, which can lead to blood loss serious enough to require blood transfusion.

A number of prescription drugs that help with cardiovascular problems interact with over-the-counter drugs and herbal supplements. Drug interactions can increase the strength of a prescription drug's impact, diminish it, or have entirely unexpected results. It is essential for anyone taking any prescription medication to educate him or herself about dangerous drug interactions.

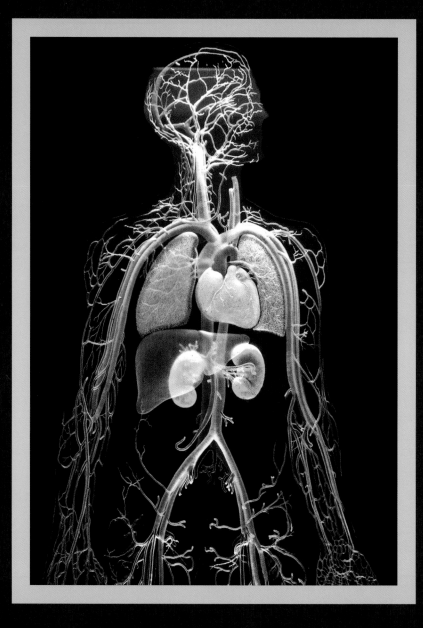

LEGAL AND ILLEGAL DRUGS, SOME OF WHICH GAIN ACCESS TO THE BLOODSTREAM VIA THE RESPIRATORY SYSTEM'S AIRWAYS, MAY HAVE DIRECT OR INDIRECT EFFECTS ON THE ABILITY TO BREATHE EFFECTIVELY.

4 DRUGS AND THE RESPIRATORY SYSTEM

The respiratory system is sometimes compared to a tree (and is sometimes called the respiratory tree). A tree's trunk, large branches, and ever smaller branches are similar to the mouth (or nose), windpipe (trachea, in the throat region), two tubes (bronchi) that branch into each of the paired lungs, and thousands of smaller branches (bronchioles) within the lungs. Like the leaves at the ends of tiny branches, bronchioles end in sacs (alveoli) where gas exchange occurs. The nervous system has some influence over the diameter of airway tubes—especially the bronchioles.

The intimate meeting of air and blood in the lungs provides a rapid way for certain drugs, such as nicotine in cigarette smoke, and inhalant drugs, such as paint thinner and gasoline fumes, to get into the bloodstream. Chemicals in tobacco and marijuana smoke, and in inhaled fumes from liquids, such as gasoline and toluene, may damage airways and lungs.

Many anesthetic medications that put someone "to sleep" for surgery enter via the respiratory system as well. Drugs that act in the brain may influence the respiratory system. Stimulants increase breathing rate, whereas depressants, including alcohol, anesthetics, and some club drugs, lower it. In fact, deaths among drug users are often caused by respiratory failure—breathing that is too slow and shallow to fuel the body with oxygen. Some over-the-counter and prescription drugs, such as allergy medications and inhalers, improve air movement through the respiratory system by reducing swelling and narrowing of the airways, which can happen with airway infections and allergies.

Normally, signals that go out from the respiratory center automatically match the body's needs for oxygen (and its need to expel carbon dioxide). Stressful situations—injury, fear, physical exertion—activate the sympathetic nervous system more than usual. This activation increases respiratory rate and depth so cells will have more oxygen to use. Relaxation, meditation, and other soothing activities decrease respiratory activity as the body rests. Drugs, too, can alter respiratory rhythm.

Route of Drug Entry

The respiratory system provides an exceedingly fast route for some kinds of drugs to get into the bloodstream. Only a very thin layer of cells in the alveoli separates air and the underlying capillaries of the bloodstream.

Powders, such as cocaine, methamphetamine, and PCP, are snorted—sniffed in through the nostrils—where the drug sticks to the moist lining of the nasal cavities and crosses into the capillaries just beneath. From there, the bloodstream carries the drug within seconds to the brain and other target organs.

Drugs in the form of inhaled smoke, gases, or vapors enter the bloodstream in this way, too. So do dozens of toxins and carcinogens in cigarette and marijuana smoke. Scientific studies have clearly linked cigarette smoking to diseases and cancer, not just of the lungs and airways but of many key organs.

Snorted powders can cause nosebleeds, loss of the sense of smell, chronic runny nose, and destruction of the nasal septum (the thin cartilage partition between nostrils). Some of the drug also reaches the back of the throat, causing sore throat, swallowing difficulty, hoarseness, and a greater chance of throat infections. Drugs that are inhaled irritate the sensitive linings of the nose, throat, or lungs. Over time, cells that are exposed to inhaled drugs and to smoke's toxins, carcinogens, and heat become

71

injured and may die, to be replaced by scar tissue that does not function as it once did.

Stimulants

Stimulant drugs, such as the amphetamines, cocaine, nicotine, and caffeine, influence the respiratory system indirectly. These stimulants increase the signals sent by the brain to muscles involved in breathing and to the airways. The result is faster, deeper breathing. The revved-up effects on the cardiovascular system can be fatal. However, medically prescribed stimulants may help people with breathing problems, such as asthma and allergic reactions, which narrow the airways and make breathing difficult.

Stimulants enhance athletic performance, especially endurance activities (those lasting more than about fifteen minutes). Even the modest stimulant caffeine was disallowed at the Olympic games for some years because of this. Stimulants aid in athletic performance in part because they increase respiratory activity.

Greater intake of oxygen and the expulsion of carbon dioxide are only part of the story. The blood must rapidly move these substances to and from cells as well. Stimulants do this, too, through their effects on the cardiovascular system.

Caffeine and its chemical relatives (the methylxanthines, such as theophylline) are relatively mild stimulants when taken as a beverage in soft drinks,

> **Stimulants' Actions on the Respiratory System**
> 1 Stimulants send excessive nerve signals from the brain to increase the rate and strength of muscle contractions involved in breathing.
> 2 Some stimulants also act directly on bronchioles to relax or widen them.
> 3 Increases in respiratory muscle action and bronchiole diameter increase air volume moving in and out of the lungs.
> 4 Oxygen and carbon dioxide exchange between air and blood is improved.

coffee, or tea. But large doses of pills or successive high-caffeine beverages ("energy" drinks) can notably speed breathing rate. Doctors take advantage of this by sometimes using caffeine, but more often theophylline, to improve breathing rhythm in premature babies whose respiratory patterns have not yet matured. In addition, doctors sometimes prescribe methylxanthines as daily medication for people with asthma, an illness in which bronchioles suddenly narrow and dangerously impede airflow in the respiratory tree.

Depressants
Depressants' effects are the opposite of stimulant effects. They slow the rhythmic inhalation and exhalation of air. In addition, depressants weaken contractions of the diaphragm and muscles of the chest wall, making each breath shallower. In this

way, alcohol, GHB, the opiates (heroin, morphine), inhaled anesthetics, and other depressant drugs deprive the brain of its usual oxygen level. In fact, depressant overdose leads to confusion, weakness, unconsciousness, coma, brain and organ damage, or death from too little oxygen.

Depressants' Actions on the Respiratory System

1 Most depressants appear to influence the respiratory system indirectly, through their actions on the brain. They enhance the GABA neurotransmitter system in the brain.

2 GABA binds to a variety of neurons and makes it more difficult for them to send messages elsewhere. In this way, GABA is a natural means of balancing overstimulation in the brain by other neurotransmitters.

3 When depressant drugs enhance GABA, this dampens the activity of many brain regions, including the respiratory center. The respiratory center therefore sends fewer signals to breathing muscles.

4 Air intake is reduced, and oxygen replenishment drops. Breathing can become so slow that oxygen uptake cannot meet the needs of the body, especially that of the brain. Grogginess, unconsciousness, coma, brain damage, and death can result.

Alcohol

Alcohol is the most common depressant drug. In a round of binge drinking, or in combination with other depressants, alcohol can kill in a matter of

74

hours. A main cause of those deaths is lack of oxygen due to respiratory system failure. Alcohol is a threat to the respiratory system in another way. It can make a person nauseated as well as sleepy—a dangerous combination if the person vomits and inhales some of the stomach contents into the airways. That can cause chemical burns (from the stomach acid) to airways and lungs and carry bacteria from the digestive tract into the airways, leading to infection. Even worse, inhalation of vomit may completely block airflow, resulting in asphyxiation.

Opiates
Opiate drugs are depressants that mimic the body's own endogenous opioid chemicals. In the brain, the drugs have a slowing, calming effect on the activity of the respiratory center. The opiate drugs used medically to relieve pain, especially morphine, have a sedative effect partly because of this depression of oxygen exchange and must be used strictly as prescribed.

Sedatives and Anesthetics
Sedatives and anesthetics, such as benzodiazepines, are depressants used to calm anxiety and to promote sleep—as well as to induce unconsciousness for surgical procedures. Barbiturates such as pentobarbital and thiopental are strong respiratory depressants still used for surgical anesthesia. Baribiturates and benzodiazepines enter the bloodstream after being swallowed as pills or injected

75

intravenously. They cross the blood-brain barrier and increase brain levels of GABA, an inhibitor of neuronal activity. Increased GABA in the respiratory center diminishes its neurons' signals to respiratory muscles. Rate and depth of breathing decreases and a state of calm, grogginess, sleep, or unconsciousness sets in. This is partly due to poorer oxygen content of blood, which brain cells need at certain levels. Overdose of these drugs can cause death by respiratory failure (insufficient oxygen delivery to the body, especially the brain).

Overdose of barbiturates, or in combination with alcohol, has caused many accidental deaths or, in some cases, suicides. Benzodiazepines, too, can contribute to life-threatening respiratory depression when combined with alcohol or other depressants, though they are less dangerous when taken alone because they don't diminish respiratory function as strongly as barbiturates do.

The drug GHB, once sold in health-food stores as a bodybuilder's supplement, is now only available legally by prescription as a treatment for a sleeping disorder. But it remains a significant drug of abuse whose depressant effects have killed people. GHB slows respiration to levels that can't sustain life. It has been discovered naturally in the brain, but its function there is not well understood. Additional GHB in drug form floods the GHB receptor system and somehow causes depression of brain activity.

Nicotine

The adverse health effects of cigarette smoking are well documented, and they are extensive. Some of the harm is short-term, such as poor oxygen binding to red blood cells because carbon monoxide (from smoke) is binding to them instead. Other problems show up over months or years of smoking. While nicotine is the highly addictive stimulant that keeps a person hooked to cigarettes, many other substances in smoke underlie most of the airway damage, smoking-related diseases, and cancers.

SMOKING INCREASES THE LUNGS' SUSCEPTIBILITY TO DAMAGE AS SHOWN IN THE SMOKER'S LUNG ON THE RIGHT. DAMAGED AIRWAY CELLS ARE LESS ABLE TO CLEAR PATHOGENS OR ALLOW THE EFFICIENT TRANSPORT OF AIR.

Hot smoke and the microscopic particles it contains irritate the airway epithelium (the moist cellular linings of the trachea, bronchi, bronchioles, and alveoli). Frequent smoking causes changes in the epithelium in the trachea. In healthy airways, tracheal cells keep inhaled particles out of the lungs by the movement of microscopic hairs, called cilia, in a direction away from the lungs. With chronic smoke irritation, those cells lose their cilia and change into a flat epithelium like that in the mouth and throat. This arrangement resists irritation better but does not keep the airways clear of inhaled particles and pathogens. As a result, smokers, as well as those who live and work with them and inhale secondhand smoke, may have airway and lung infections more often, and become sicker with them, than nonsmokers.

Cigarette smoking is the leading cause of lung diseases, such as pneumonia, bronchitis, and emphysema, which account for close to a million deaths annually in the United States. Each of these diseases involves damage to the cellular lining of the airways because of recurrent irritation by substances in tobacco smoke. Pneumonia is an infection of the lungs by pathogens (usually bacteria and viruses). Bronchitis is an infection of the bronchi, which carry air to the lungs.

Emphysema is an irreversible, fatal illness in which the tissues of the lungs are gradually destroyed. Unfortunately, people do not have symptoms of emphysema until about a third of lung tissue is permanently damaged. Then a serious recurring cough, shortness of breath, or chest pain can send them to the doctor. Smoking is most often the cause of emphysema. Inhaled particles and many foreign chemicals in smoke settle into the alveoli, where immune cells release enzymes to destroy them. With chronic smoke inhalation and ongoing activation of immune cells, lung tissue is repeatedly irritated by the enzymes and is gradually replaced by scar tissue. Over time, whole regions of the lung are transformed into large bubbles devoid of elastic tissue. Bronchioles in the area collapse, and virtually no gas exchange can occur. Eventually someone with emphysema requires around-the-clock oxygen to stay alive. This end stage may go on for years. The patient grows increasingly weak, then dies from the condition.

Cigarette smoking is thought to be responsible for a third of *all* cancers among the population in the United States. A person who smokes is twice as likely to die from some form of cancer than a non-smoker, and four times as likely if he or she is a heavy smoker. Many are cancers of the airways and areas exposed directly to smoke: the mouth, tongue, lips, salivary glands, throat, larynx, and lungs. About 90 percent of lung cancer cases are due to smoking. Smokeless tobacco (chewing tobacco and snuff) also causes cancer of the mouth, including lips, tongue, cheeks, gums, and the floor or roof of the mouth. Tobacco smoke is listed as a known carcinogen by the federal government. Altogether, airway cancers kill about 170,000 people a year. Substances in tobacco smoke also are associated with higher rates of cancer in other organs, such as the stomach, pancreas, kidney, bladder, uterus, cervix, and others.

Dozens of toxins and cancer-causing substances exist in cigarette smoke, smokeless tobacco, and marijuana. The particles in smoke include PAHs (polycyclic aromatic hydrocarbons), nitrosamines, and other substances—at least fifty of which are proven to mutate DNA and to cause cancer in laboratory animals. PAHs and nitrosamines from tobacco smoke (and from other smoked plant materials) enter cells and attach to DNA.

The DNA/chemical complex is called an adduct. DNA that is part of an adduct cannot function properly—it is mutated. Adducts have been measured in samples of cells from the lungs of smokers and are significantly more abundant than in cells of nonsmokers. People who have quit smoking have fewer adducts than smokers. This suggests that DNA damage to lung cells is reversible, at least if cancer has not yet developed.

Smoke contains carbon monoxide, which enters the bloodstream and diffuses into red blood cells. There it binds to hemoglobin, the iron-containing protein that carries oxygen throughout the body for cells' needs. Carbon monoxide attaches more strongly to hemoglobin than oxygen does, lowering the amount of oxygen that red blood cells can carry. Carbon monoxide in cigarette (or marijuana) smoke can be dangerous to people who already have health problems that reduce oxygen delivery to tissues, such as poor circulation, iron deficiency, and heart or lung disease. Also, carbon monoxide inhalation from secondhand smoke can poison infants and fetuses (via carbon monoxide in the mother's blood).

Tobacco smoke is dangerous for nonsmokers, too. This secondhand smoke, also called environmental tobacco smoke, is estimated to cause about three thousand lung cancer deaths among nonsmokers each year in the United States. The Environmen-tal Protection Agency lists secondhand smoke as a known human lung carcinogen. People who live with a smoker are more likely to develop asthma and have worse symptoms than people from a smoke-free home. Breathing secondhand smoke is also associated with more colds and sore throats, as well as bronchitis and pneumonia.

Children are especially susceptible to airway irritation from secondhand smoke. Each year between 150,000 to 300,000 children under eighteen months of age who live with a smoker get lung infections. Between 7,500 and 15,000 of these children are hospitalized. Ear infection rates are higher in children who live in a home with a smoker. This occurs because inhaled smoke irritates eustachian tubes, which connect the throat with the middle ear. The tubes become swollen and narrowed, trapping bacteria in the middle ear. Secondhand smoke has even been implicated in about 2,000 cases of SIDS (sudden infant death syndrome) annually.

Marijuana
Marijuana's most important impacts on the respiratory system are through smoke. Unlike the health hazards of tobacco smoking, those of frequent or long-term marijuana smoking have received relatively little study. This is due to the illegality of the substance. It is known that smoke from any source irritates the tissues in mouth, airways, and lungs, making the airways more susceptible to lung infections and disease. And burning marijuana contains many potentially harmful substances. These substances pass into capillaries in the lungs and into the bloodstream to be distributed throughout the body.

Some harmful components are more concentrated in marijuana smoke than in cigarette smoke (cigarette filters remove some of them). Marijuana smokers further increase their exposure because they tend to hold marijuana smoke in the lungs longer than cigarette smoke. This long inhalation extends the time that toxins can enter cells and the bloodstream. Overall, potential harm from marijuana smoke is poorly studied.

Inhalants

The respiratory tract is the route of entry for the inhalants, a diverse group of gases, vapors (evaporated liquids), and aerosols (sprays). Most abused inhalants are vapors from glues, paint thinners, cleaners, lighter fluid, gasoline, and other fuels.

A person takes an inhalant into the lungs by deeply breathing gases or vapors from volatile liquids. Within seconds, they cross into capillaries. Once in the bloodstream, inhalants are carried throughout the body. In the brain, many act as depressants, including on the respiratory center. Overdose can lead to respiratory failure and death. Inhalant use can also cause life-threatening disruption of oxygen delivery because the inhaled vapors replace air—and its life-sustaining oxygen—in the lungs. Inhalants can also kill if the user becomes nauseated or vomits in reaction to the drug and then accidentally inhales vomit that blocks the airways.

Besides the depressant effect on breathing, inhalants are very dangerous to the airways. Some people inhale vapors from pressurized containers, such as aerosol spray cans or propane tanks, without realizing that when the gas is released from the container, it instantly expands. If a person has inhaled directly from the canister, the expanding gas can severely damage the lungs by rupturing bronchioles and alveoli, or even an entire lung. In addition, the expanding gases become dramatically

83

cooler—enough so that cells lining the airways can be destroyed by the freezing temperature. Further, a user can suffocate if he or she is inhaling vapor from a plastic bag in an attempt to concentrate the drug and heighten the amount entering the lungs. If the person passes out with the bag covering the nose and mouth, he or she can die of suffocation.

Over-the-Counter Airway Aids

Some of the most common medicines target the airways. Cold, flu, and allergy (hay fever) remedies contain drugs with many actions on the airways: drying up runny nose, reducing airway inflammation (swelling), stifling the urge to cough, and reducing pain of sore throat and aching sinuses. A key ingredient in these remedies is an antihistamine—a drug that blocks the action of histamine. Histamine is a naturally occurring chemical with many effects, including some that hamper respiration. For instance, histamine attaches to capillaries and increases their permeability. This allows fluid to escape the bloodstream into surrounding tissues. And while that is a normal (and essential) way in which blood-borne substances penetrate cells, too much histamine causes excessive fluid accumulation in tissues. In the nose, throat, and airways, excess histamine causes watery eyes, runny nose, cough, and congestion (narrowed, clogged airways). Histamine also binds to smooth muscle cells around bronchioles, causing them to contract. That narrows the bronchioles, impeding airflow.

84

Histamine is released by airway cells when they are irritated and inflamed by smoke, bacteria, viruses, or allergens such as pollen and animal dander. Antihistamines reduce symptoms by diminishing capillary leakiness and bronchiole narrowing. Many antihistamines cause drowsiness and should not be taken before someone drives, operates machinery, or does dangerous physical tasks. Antihistamines must not be combined with central nervous system depressants. The combination may dangerously lower breathing and heart rate.

Certain over-the-counter products are sprayed into the nostrils or inhaled more deeply into the lungs. Examples are nose drops and nasal sprays that contain antihistamines to reduce swelling and dry up runny nose and watery eyes. Other products give immediate breathing assistance to people with asthma, an illness in which bronchiole muscle narrows. Pocket-size devices called inhalers deliver a premeasured dose of a bronchodilator drug, which relaxes bronchiole muscles rapidly.

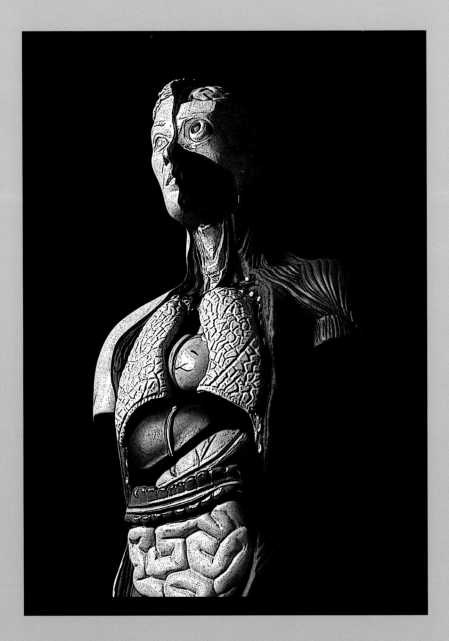

THE DIGESTIVE SYSTEM IS A KEY ROUTE OF ENTRY FOR MANY LEGAL AND ILLEGAL DRUGS. CERTAIN DRUGS ACT DIRECTLY ON THE DIGESTIVE TRACT. SOME RELIEVE AILMENTS. OTHERS CAUSE SERIOUS DIGESTIVE REACTIONS OR INJURY.

5 DRUGS AND THE DIGESTIVE SYSTEM

Although digestion may seem a simple matter of taking in foods and liquids and ridding waste from the body, the digestive process is highly complex. To some degree, the brain and nerves of the autonomic nervous system (the subset of nerves that provides unconscious regulation of internal organs) control the movement of food and its digestion. Additionally, a network of nerves within the digestive system itself connects its different regions and is essential to proper digestion.

The digestive system can be likened to a factory assembly line—only in reverse. Instead of assembling something, the digestive tract breaks it into pieces. That "something" consists of food and beverages. A food item, such as a sandwich, is taken in bite-sized pieces into the mouth, crushed by the teeth, and swallowed. It then travels through the esophagus, stomach, small intestine, and large intestine. Along that journey digestive enzymes disassemble the sandwich into molecules. Molecules that are of use to the body are absorbed into the bloodstream and distributed wherever blood goes. Those molecules that cannot be absorbed, such as undigested plant matter, are defecated as waste.

Many drugs gain entry to the body through the digestive tract. Some drugs of abuse can interfere with digestion or with hunger and nutrition. On the other hand, several types of over-the-counter drugs are intended to assist in digestion or alleviate symptoms of illness that disrupt digestion.

Drug dependence disrupts proper eating habits. Eating creates surges in serotonin, dopamine, and endogenous opioids in the brain, including in the pleasure circuit. Certain drugs also create surges in these chemicals, or mimic them. Many drugs of abuse have a special link with the digestive tract because they activate the pleasure circuit, too.

Most of the time digestion goes on without conscious awareness or thought about it. But sometimes, digestive turmoil such as pain, nausea, diarrhea, constipation, heartburn, and intestinal gas can be disruptive, annoying, or even quite painful. Illicit drugs can cause such problems, whereas certain over-the-counter drugs help to control them. Some psychoactive drugs, known for their influence on the brain, are structurally related to chemicals that regulate digestion. Researchers continue to explore how such drugs might act on digestion directly instead of indirectly, through the brain.

Route of Drug Entry
The digestive tract is the site of entry into the body for many kinds of medications and some illicit drugs. Certain drugs need go no further than the mouth to have an effect. Nicotine gum is an example. When chewed, it releases nicotine that is absorbed across the moist lining of the mouth, delivering a dose into the bloodstream and reducing nicotine craving in people who are trying to stop smoking. Many mouthwashes contain drugs to kill germs in the mouth. Most toothpastes contain fluoride, intended to toughen tooth enamel. Herbal tinctures (plant extracts dissolved in alcohol) are dropped under the tongue for absorption. Even a condition as serious as heart attack can be thwarted in some people with heart disease by placing tablets of nitroglycerin under the tongue at the first sign of pain. From there it is absorbed into the bloodstream and converted to nitric oxide, which acts on blood vessels to improve blood flow—all within a few minutes.

However, most medications and drugs someone takes by mouth are absorbed across the intestinal lining and into the bloodstream. Many prescription and over-the-counter drugs are enclosed in special coatings that withstand the stomach's harsh environment, so the drug arrives in the intestine intact. Some products, though, simply include a larger quantity of drug, allowing for a certain amount to be lost to stomach digestion.

Drugs of abuse can have a different impact on a user when taken orally instead of being smoked, snorted, or injected. A drug that is swallowed takes longer to get into the bloodstream than if the drug were injected or snorted. Food in the digestive tract slows absorption of a drug even further. As a result, blood concentrations of a drug taken orally are usually lower, and its effects weaker, than other routes of delivery. For example, when taken orally, the stimulant methamphetamine influences the central nervous system in about fifteen or twenty minutes. The drug creates a sense of happiness that lasts many minutes or even hours. When injected or smoked, however, methamphetamine creates an intense surge of pleasurable sensations that begins within seconds and dissipates rapidly.

Stimulants

Stimulant drugs typically depress hunger. They boost the body's energy resources by stimulating the sympathetic nervous system. One of that system's actions is to mobilize stored fat for energy. With those fat molecules in the bloodstream, the person does not feel hungry.

Although taking stimulants may sound like a good way to lose weight, they rarely lead to long-

> **Stimulants' Actions on the Digestive System**
> 1 Many stimulant drugs are taken orally and cross the cells of the intestine into nearby capillaries.
>
> 2 Once in the bloodstream, stimulants enter the brain and activate the sympathetic nervous system, where its neurons rev up brain and body activities by secreting norepinephrine.
>
> 3 Norepinephrine (and hence the drug) enhances the ability of fat cells to get their stored fats into the bloodstream.
>
> 4 Elevated quantities of fats in the bloodstream provide energy for bodily activities without the need to eat and also diminish the sensation of hunger within the brain's hunger center.
>
> 5 Stimulants' influences on hunger wear off as the drug is metabolized into inactive forms by the liver and excreted in urine.

term weight loss. As stimulant effects wear off, a rebound drop in blood fats and a renewed sensation of hunger can undermine a dieter's willpower, leading to excessive eating.

Amphetamines
Amphetamines' combined effects subdue the urge to eat while boosting energy. They do this by mimicking the actions of norepinephrine, a brain chemical that stimulates a person's energy level and gets stored fats into the bloodstream. Amphetamines are also similar in chemical composition to epinephrine, another natural stimulant, and to dopamine.

91

These drugs also appear to cause a surge in serotonin levels in the brain, as eating does. All the chemicals with which amphetamines interact are either neurotransmitters of the pleasure circuit or involved in hunger, eating, and the body's energy supplies.

Amphetamine users may take the drugs in several ways: by mouth, injection, or inhalation through the nose—snorting. The drugs then travel to the brain, influence several neurotransmitter systems related to eating, and stimulate dopamine in the pleasure center, which may explain their addictive nature. When amphetamines are metabolized by the liver and excreted in urine, a user may feel depleted of energy and extremely hungry.

Not surprisingly, amphetamine-based drugs became popular as weight-loss drugs, especially in the 1960s, because they heightened energy while suppressing appetite. But they had a serious side effect: dependence. Since then, pharmaceutical companies have developed other products based on amphetamines but without the addictive qualities. These drugs stimulate the serotonin neurotransmitter system (as does food intake) but don't influence the dopamine system, which is strongly implicated in dependency.

Cocaine
Cocaine shares many of amphetamines' characteristics, including an ability to stave off hunger. But it can lead to dependence. People who are heavily

dependent on cocaine will spend time and money on their next "fix" rather than on food. In fact, it is common for cocaine-dependent users to become malnourished, underweight, and prone to illnesses because they stop eating properly.

Cocaine users snort, smoke, or inject cocaine. The drug then travels through the bloodstream. When it reaches the brain, cocaine enhances neurotransmitters of the pleasure circuit, especially dopamine. Like amphetamines, cocaine also appears to mimic the actions of norepinephrine, which stimulates a person's energy level and releases stored fats into the bloodstream. Because cocaine subdues the sensation of hunger and also creates a craving for the drug through actions on the pleasure circuit, a user's drug-seeking and drug-taking behaviors take priority over eating. Cocaine's short-term dampening of hunger wears off when the drug is metabolized by the liver and excreted in urine.

Nicotine

Nicotine is well known to curb hunger. Cigarette smokers typically gain weight when they quit. In fact, some smokers say that a fear of gaining weight is one reason they will not quit, and some start up again as pounds accumulate. Although it isn't yet clear why, nicotine is a hunger suppressant, possibly through its general stimulant properties. Nicotine enters the brain, where it acts as a stimulant, enhancing the sensation of energy and blocking sensations of hunger.

Caffeine

Caffeine is included in some weight-loss products. Although currently thought to be generally harmless except in very large amounts, caffeine may not be of much help in weight loss over the long run. When caffeine is consumed in coffee, for example, the beverage stimulates digestive activity. That, in turn, signals the brain that the digestive tract is ready for food. And, as with other stimulants, a "crash," or energy low, follows a caffeine high. To overcome that low, a person may choose a high-sugar, high-fat snack, with its many calories.

Depressants

The influence of depressant drugs on the digestive system is not as conspicuous as that of stimulants. A depressant that sedates a person will also reduce his or her awareness of hunger and desire to eat, at least in the short term. Alcohol is best known for its impact on eating and nutrition. In excess, alcohol consumption causes weight gain and poor physical activity levels. Heavy alcohol drinking can lead to malnutrition, too, as alcoholic beverages, with few nutrients, replace nutritious meals. Even moderate drinkers may gain weight from a favorite alcoholic beverage because the alcohol itself (ethanol) is a carbohydrate and contributes calories, just as foods do.

As soon as alcohol enters the bloodstream, the liver begins to break it down into inactive forms.

94

But liver cells can only handle so much at a time. The average adult's liver can metabolize approximately 8 to 10 grams of ethanol an hour (about 10 ounces of regular beer, 3-4 ounces of wine, or 1 ounce of hard liquor). If a person drinks too much too quickly, unmetabolized ethanol passes into the bloodstream, carrying it to the brain and causing intoxication.

The most profound effects of alcohol on the digestive tract take time to show up. Long-term excessive alcohol consumption can lead to obesity due to ethanol's caloric content, or malnutrition due to poor eating habits during long periods of intoxication.

Alcoholic hepatitis, caused by excessive, long-term alcohol consumption, is a condition in which the liver is inflamed and painful, and its cells are injured. The cells function poorly, allowing cellular waste products they normally remove to accumulate in the bloodstream and tissues. One such waste product is bilirubin (from old red blood cells), which gives a yellowish tinge to the skin and whites of the eyes—a condition called jaundice. People can recover from alcoholic hepatitis when the overconsumption stops. But chronic ethanol consumption can also lead to cirrhosis, in which large areas of liver cells die and are replaced by scar tissue and fat. Only a liver transplant can save the life of a person with severe cirrhosis.

Opiates

Opiates, such as morphine used for pain relief after surgery, are especially known to slow or stop digestive activities. Constipation is one of the most troubling digestive-system side effects of prescribed depressants. After major surgery, for example, a patient may go for many hours or days before normal intestinal contractions start up again. Nausea, too, is a problem for many people taking opiates. Additional drugs can help offset constipation and reduce nausea.

Cells in the digestive tract have receptors for opioid molecules whether they come in drugs or in the body's naturally occurring opioids, such as endorphins. That suggests opioids participate in digestive tract activities. But the digestive upset caused by opioid drugs is one piece of evidence that the opioid chemical system is important in controlling the contraction and relaxation of muscles that keep food moving along the tract.

Marijuana

Today, researchers are finding cannabinoid receptors in the digestive tract. These receptors suggest a possible mechanism for the effect that THC has on the digestive tract muscle, and perhaps its immune cells. After marijuana is inhaled in smoke (and occasionally in food prepared with marijuana), the THC in marijuana travels in the bloodstream to the brain. There it attaches to cannabinoid receptors in many regions, including in the hunger/satiety center, where it stimulates the urge to eat. The drug's effects wear off as the liver metabolizes it into inactive forms that are cleared by the kidneys and excreted in urine.

Researchers are studying marijuana and drugs based on THC (in laboratory animals and people) as treatments for diseases of the digestive tract that involve inflammation, such as ulcers, irritable bowel syndrome, Crohn's disease, and gastroesophageal reflux (heartburn).

Marijuana users joke about getting "the munchies" while under the drug's influence. And medical researchers have proven that marijuana does, in fact, stimulate hunger. Scientists have created medications based on THC (marijuana's best-studied psychoactive ingredient) to improve appetite in people with illnesses, such as cancer or AIDS, that interfere with appetite.

Drugs and Liver Damage
The liver is extremely important in ending a drug's effects. Its cells metabolize all kinds of drugs and toxins, changing them into inactive forms. That includes medications, which the liver inactivates into useless forms (though sometimes it creates a metabolite that still has a beneficial effect).

But the liver can be damaged by pathogens (bacteria and viruses), cancer, and even the toxins it metabolizes. If there is enough damage, the liver cannot metabolize drugs as well. As a result, a drug will remain active longer in someone with liver damage than in someone with a healthy liver. The recommended dosing for prescription and over-the-counter drugs assumes that a person has a healthy liver, which will metabolize the drug at a certain rate. People with poor liver function can accidentally overdose if a drug is still circulating when they take the next dose(s). Warning labels on many medications specify they are not to be taken by people with liver problems. But some people only discover they have liver disease when adverse reactions to a drug appear.

Infants and young children metabolize sub-stances more slowly, too, because their livers are still maturing. This is one of the reasons a medication must never be given to a child unless its label says it is safe for children. Even something as common-place as caffeine is metabolized much more slowly in children. As such, the effects of a single beverage last longer, and several beverages throughout the day can create much higher circulating levels of caf-feine in children than in adults.

Over-the-Counter Digestive Aids

A host of over-the-counter products help with dis-comforts of the digestive tract, such as heartburn, cramps, nausea, diarrhea, and constipation. Most of these products are a welcome aid for temporary problems. However, recurrent digestive problems or

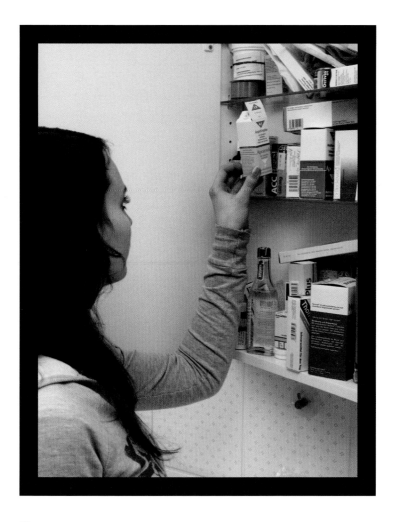

OVER-THE-COUNTER AND PRESCRIBED MEDICATIONS CARRY WARNINGS ABOUT WELL-KNOWN DRUG INTERACTIONS, SIDE EFFECTS, AND POTENTIAL ALLERGIC REACTIONS. UPDATES ON DRUG INTERACTIONS CAN BE FOUND THROUGH A DOCTOR, PHARMACIST, OR WEB SITES OF DRUG MANUFACTURERS.

intense pain should be checked out by a doctor. They may signal a serious illness—or simply mean that eating behaviors or food choices need changing.

Nonprescription Pain Relievers

Some of the most popular digestive aids ease the pain of stomachache, heartburn (acid reflux), or intestinal cramps. These nonprescription pain relievers are usually NSAIDs—nonsteroidal anti-inflammatory drugs, such as aspirin and acetaminophen. They block the cellular production of substances called prostaglandins, which have many purposes. Their presence in the body contributes to the sensation of pain carried by neurons to the brain. Within the digestive tract itself, prostaglandins are necessary for making mucus that protects cells from damage by stomach acid. Long-term or high-dose OTC pain relievers can lead to digestive tract injury and bleeding due to low mucus production. Frequent or high doses of NSAIDs, especially aspirin, can lead to stomach irritation and bleeding. The bleeding can be a small amount at a time but over weeks or months can dangerously reduce the number of red blood cells. Sometimes the injury is severe enough that blood vessels rupture, requiring emergency medical attention.

Antacids

Antacids are products that neutralize stomach acid. People take them for heartburn, a searing pain in the chest that comes from the place where the esophagus meets the stomach. Also known as GERD (gastroesophageal reflux disease), the condition is more common in people who are overweight in the abdomen. The extra pounds create pressure

Digestive Tract: A Second Brain?

The digestive tract has actually been called "the second brain" by researchers. One of them, Michael Gershon, wrote a book by that name. For decades, he and many other scientists have been discovering that, as in the brain, cells in digestive tract intercommunicate with neurotransmitters and other chemical messengers to influence each other's activities. Several of those chemicals are also found in the brain. Serotonin, endogenous cannabinoids, and endogenous opiates are among them. In fact, serotonin is far more abundant in the digestive tract than in the brain. Released in response to a meal, serotonin stimulates peristalsis (muscular contractions that move food along the digestive tract) and the secretion of digestive juices in the intestine. It also stimulates nerves that carry messages to the brain, indicating how full the tract is. It is interesting that serotonin, and probably the endogenous cannabinoids, control activities related to food in both the brain and digestive tract.

that pushes some of the stomach contents into the lower portion of the esophagus, irritating the cells. But GERD can be due to certain medications, pregnancy, or to a malformation in the esophageal-stomach juncture.

Substances in the antacid product, often magnesium or aluminum, neutralize stomach acid. These may be absorbed to some degree by intestinal cells and transported into the bloodstream. Lower acidity reduces acid-induced pain in stomach or intestine tissues. However, overuse of antacids reduces food breakdown and nutrient availability. Antacid components that are not absorbed into the bloodstream are lost from the body in feces.

While antacid use seems harmless and relieves short-term discomfort, there are a couple of dangers to their use. Neutralizing stomach acid makes food digestion less efficient. This inefficiency increases the chances that pathogens survive the stomach and move on into the intestine, where an infection may arise. In addition, "heartburn" may actually be pain emanating from the heart when its oxygen supply is poor—a condition that precedes a heart attack.

Constipation and Diarrhea Medications
Several over-the-counter digestive products treat constipation or diarrhea—the opposite conditions of too little or too much bowel activity. Constipation ("irregularity" in advertising lingo) means that bowel

movements are infrequent and fecal material is unusually solid. It can result from insufficient fiber (indigestible plant materials) in the diet, illnesses, or certain medications and drugs that inhibit peristalsis, the movement of food along the digestive tract. Remedies are called laxatives or stool softeners. Some simply add substances that make feces moist and easier to pass, while others enhance peristalsis.

Diarrhea is the problem of bowel movements that are too frequent, so that fecal material contains water that should have been absorbed in the large intestine. Diarrhea is most often caused by infection of the digestive tract by bacteria, viruses, or other microorganisms. The infection activates immune cells in the digestive tract. Those cells, in their efforts to kill the microorganisms, release histamine, a chemical that triggers digestive muscle to contract. That moves materials along the tract too rapidly for much water to be absorbed. Water loss because of diarrhea can leave tissues dehydrated enough to be fatal. (Indeed, diarrhea is one of the most common causes of death worldwide, especially among children who live in villages that have poor sanitation so that intestinal pathogens are easily spread.) Over-the-counter products can halt diarrhea by weakening muscle activity, though doing so also slows the body's ability to expel pathogens in feces. Therefore, their use to treat diarrhea should be temporary.

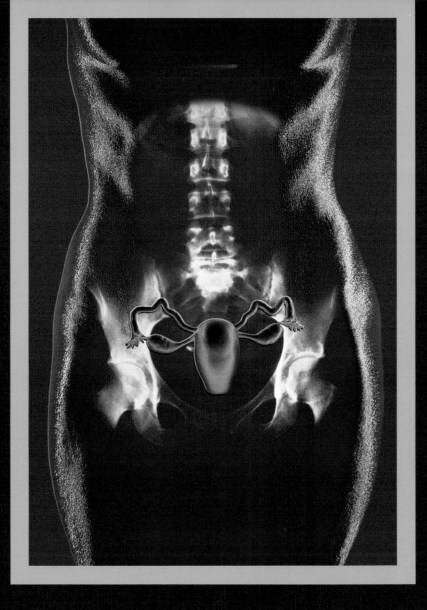

Drugs that influence behavior and mood can also modify sexual behavior and affect the reproductive system. Other drugs, such as anabolic steroids and birth control drugs, directly disrupt the reproductive system by mimicking its hormones. In addition, drugs are exceptionally dangerous to a fetus or infant.

6 DRUGS AND THE REPRODUCTIVE SYSTEM

The reproductive system is the only system of the body that is not essential for an individual's survival (in contrast to the cardiovascular system, for example). However, it is essential for the survival of the species. The system's primary function is to create offspring. Additionally, the reproductive system produces steroid hormones that interact with many of the body's cells and tissues to ensure proper growth and good health. Those hormones act on sexual organs during puberty and cause the emergence of sexual characteristics of males and females, both physically and behaviorally.

Drugs can influence the reproductive system directly and indirectly. For instance, birth control drugs directly block the maturation of eggs in women or the ability of a man's sperm to fertilize an egg. On the other hand, psychoactive drugs, such as stimulants, may increase a person's desire to have sexual experiences. Antidepressants may dampen desire. In pregnant women, the fetus is susceptible to effects—both predictable and unpredictable—of virtually any drug in the mother's bloodstream when drugs cross the placenta and get into the fetus's bloodstream.

Natural Reproductive Steroids
The gonads of men and women make many steroid hormones. They fall into three main groups: progestins, androgens, and estrogens. All the steroids share a molecular structure called a steroid nucleus. Progestins are precursor molecules from which gonadal cells make androgens. Androgens are precursors to estrogens.

Ovaries and testes both make progestins, androgens, and estrogens. But the relative quantity of each steroid type in the bloodstream differs between men and women. Men have high androgen levels and very low levels of the others, whereas women have high estrogen levels (and high progestins during some phases of the menstrual cycle) but very low androgens. These relative proportions of steroids account for male versus female characteristics.

In women, estrogens released by ovaries stimulate development of breasts and external genitalia during puberty. Then, in a sexually mature female, a monthly surge of estrogens and progestins from the ovaries stimulates growth of the uterine lining, enriching its glandular secretions and blood supply in case a fertilized egg settles into the uterus that month as a result of sexual intercourse. In the absence of fertilization, levels of estrogens and progestins drop, triggering the uterus to shed some of its lining (menstrual flow). Estrogens also enhance female sexual desire and behavior by interacting with brain cells.

In men, androgens released by testes stimulate development of male external genitalia. These androgens also stimulate the development of other physical characteristics during puberty, including a male pattern of body hair, deeper voice (by enlargement of the voice box), increased muscle mass, and typically male skeletal features (eyebrow ridges, wider jaw, larger frame). Androgens further enhance male sexual desire by interacting with brain cells.

Steroids and other hormones that travel in the bloodstream affect communication between gonads and the brain. These hormones act like messengers that monitor steroid levels so they don't get too high or too low. Together, the cells in the gonads and brain form a long-distance network that maintains proper steroid levels, and hence healthy reproductive function.

Changes in steroid balances may change physical appearances. These changes may come about in several ways. Steroid-based drugs, genetic disorders, or steroid-producing tumors of the gonads or adrenals (which also produce steroids) may alter the balance of natural steroids in the body. For instance, androgen-based drugs can cause beard growth in a woman by overwhelming her estrogens. A genetic error in a man that prevents his cells from reacting properly to his natural androgens will block beard growth and maturation of his genitals.

Both illegal and prescribed drugs can affect the reproductive system negatively or positively. For instance, contraceptive drugs inhibit a woman's ability to produce a mature egg, whereas certain prescription drugs augment her hormones to encourage egg production.

Drugs may also act directly or indirectly. Muscle-building steroids mimic androgens and disrupt normal steroid balance in both men and women. Psychoactive drugs, such as stimulants, depressants, and antidepressants, can indirectly affect the reproductive system by altering sexual behavior. Even the act of sharing needles and syringes to inject drugs is related to reproduction. These practices may spread deadly diseases, such as viral hepatitis and human immunodeficiency virus, or HIV, which are further spread sexually.

Another interface between drugs and reproduction occurs when a woman uses drugs while pregnant or nursing a baby. Alcohol, for example, can cause lifelong brain damage to a fetus if the mother drinks during pregnancy. A pregnant or nursing woman must avoid virtually all drugs and medications, and even herbal products, to protect the fetus or developing infant from possible drug-induced harm.

Many drugs influence the choices a person makes in social settings. A glass of wine can relax one's nerves while on a date. A high-caffeine energy drink can fuel a long night of dancing at the club. Both scenarios may increase the chances of becoming intimate. While that can be pleasant and safe, drug use is well known to cloud judgment and increase the chances of unplanned or unwanted sex and unprotected intercourse. That in turn can cause pregnancy or transmission of diseases, for example, HIV, genital warts, hepatitis, and herpes, as well as negative emotional and social consequences of unplanned sexual behavior.

Stimulants

Stimulants, especially in high doses, give a kick of energy that can last through the night. People who attend all-night dance parties, or raves, are often fueled by caffeine-laden energy drinks, amphetamines, or cocaine. When revved up with stimulants, they may have exaggerated feelings of power and aggressiveness—including the pursuit of someone for sex. Stimulants also boost energy for sexual activity when the body's natural energy levels would be waning and calling for sleep.

Cocaine users, in addition to sensing the drug's stimulant effects, have likened the surge of sensations immediately following an injected or snorted dose to sexual orgasm. For severely dependent people, cocaine highs sometimes replace normal interest in sexual activities. On the other hand, cocaine and increased sexual activity are linked, too, because a user might have sex in exchange for a drug fix or for money to buy drugs.

Depressants

Alcohol and other depressants can have mixed effects on reproductive behavior. They lower a person's inhibitions, subdue awareness, and cloud judgment. All of these effects may increase sexual encounters and unwise practices, such as having intercourse without using a condom. Depressants that are used as "date rape" drugs—Rohypnol, GHB, ketamine, and other sedatives—are dangerous not just because of their depressant effects on breathing and heart rate but because of reproductive consequences for the victim. A female rape victim who ingests one of these drugs may become pregnant. A victim of either gender may become infected with sexually transmitted diseases.

People who are addicted to depressants may, however, have little or no interest in sex. Chronic heavy drinkers have reported a loss of sexual desire. Moreover, alcohol-addicted men have problems reaching and maintaining an erection. Their sperm count may be lower than normal.

Anabolic Steroids

Anabolic steroids are well known to increase sexual behavior and aggression in men by flooding the

110

brain with androgens, which stimulate male sexual desire and other typically male behaviors. Steroids don't act right away but instead build in effect over weeks and months of consumption. Many steroid users report increasing feelings of sexual drive, aggression, and emotional volatility—a combination that has led to rape and violence from otherwise reasonable men.

Steroids can have significant effects on the development of sexual traits. Although a person's chromosomal makeup determines sex at birth, the steroid hormones that are later produced by his or her gonads have immense impact on physical traits. Gender-specific features, such as beard growth, shape and size of certain bones, and degree of muscular build, all are under steroid hormone control. Because of this, of all the drugs that affect the reproductive system, anabolic steroids have the most direct effect on traits. They are similar in molecular structure to the predominant reproductive steroid in men's bloodstreams, testosterone. Testosterone is an androgen. It spurs the appearance of many male traits, including muscle growth. (It does so in women as well, but to a lesser degree because women normally have low testosterone levels.)

Anabolic steroids are available legally through a doctor's prescription for certain medical conditions, such as abnormally low natural androgen production. But there is a vibrant illegal market for anabolic steroids that supplies bodybuilders and athletes with the drug. The more common anabolic steroids

SOME MEN AND WOMEN INTERESTED IN SCULPTING THEIR BODIES TAKE ANABOL-IC STEROIDS ORALLY OR BY INJECTION. TYPICAL DOSES PRODUCE BLOODSTREAM CONCENTRATIONS OF TESTOSTERONE-LIKE ANDROGENS THAT ARE MUCH HIGHER THAN WOULD EVER OCCUR NATURALLY.

go by the brand names Anadrol, Superdrol, Oxandrin, Dianabol, Winstrol, Deca Durabolin, and Boldenone. Some are actually veterinary products (for animals). Sometimes bodybuilding supplements contain steroids.

Muscle building may seem harmless enough, but doctors have grave concerns about the side effects of steroids at such high doses. Anabolic steroids are

112

especially designed to build muscle. They are a poor replacement for testosterone produced naturally by testes. In fact, anabolic steroids cause infertility and "shrinking" testes. This happens because they act as a powerful negative feedback on brain regions that support activity in the testes. With the brain's stimulus gone, testes stop producing testosterone and sperm. Men may also experience gynecomastia (growth of breast tissue) and balding as their own testosterone plummets and the drugs are metabolized within the body into atypical steroids (such as estrogens) with unexpected and varied effects.

Women who take anabolic steroids are flooding their systems with androgens, which normally never happens. They may lose hair on the head but grow excessive hair elsewhere, including on the chest and face. They may develop deeper voices, because androgens enlarge the larynx (voice box), which changes the timbre of the voice. Their clitoris may become enlarged. Menstrual cycles become erratic or cease.

Both men and women may get severe acne, become infertile, or develop liver and kidney tumors. Anabolic steroids are linked to high blood pressure and altered blood lipids, which increase the risk of heart problems. What's more, extreme mood swings and aggression are common.

Many of these changes in an adult's body are reversible, though it may take months or years after the drugs are stopped for the body to return to normal. However, not all the effects of anabolic steroid use among young people are reversible. Naturally produced steroids help to complete a young person's bone growth at the end of puberty. But young people who use anabolic steroids during puberty reach sexual maturation sooner and may have stunted growth. Studies have documented that, on average, steroid users are shorter as adults than peers who did not use steroids.

Increasingly, some children who have not even begun puberty are taking anabolic steroids. Such young users start puberty earlier than normal and become sexually interested sooner than their peers. That increases the child's chances of acquiring sexually transmitted diseases, creating unwanted pregnancies early in life, and stunting his or her growth.

Hallucinogens, Inhalants, and Dissociatives

Drugs that alter perception of reality can, like stimulants and depressants, change how a person perceives a social situation or personal interaction. Hallucinogens and dissociative drugs disconnect a person from an accurate understanding of what is going on. A person under the influence of marijuana, for instance, may feel more relaxed, happier, playful, and more open to another person than usual, which might lead to unplanned sexual intimacy. In addition, any drug that reduces a person's ability to make decisions or replaces muscular coordination with lethargy and weakness, as inhalants can, heightens vulnerability to sexual abuse.

Antidepressants

Certain antidepressants, intended to improve a person's mood, have the common side effect of dampening sexual interest. How they do so is not completely understood, but it may involve the important brain neurotransmitter serotonin. Antidepressants that elevate serotonin levels, such as the selective serotonin reuptake inhibitors (SSRIs) Paxil, Prozac, and Zoloft, typically diminish sexual interest. When these drugs are discontinued and wear off over a few weeks, sexual desire returns (unless the depression returns, too).

Fetal and Infant Health

Alcohol can seriously damage a developing fetus. It is clearly responsible for permanent brain damage and other problems of development. Fetal alcohol syndrome is a group of physical deformities and disabilities, including severe mental retardation, linked to heavy alcohol consumption by mothers.

Even moderate drinking—one or two alcoholic beverages a day while pregnant—is associated with intellectual and behavioral problems in the child that can last into adulthood. Termed fetal alcohol effects, these problems include hyperactivity and inability to focus on tasks for long—as in ADHD (attention deficit hyperactivity disorder)—and poor scores on tests of schooling basics: reading, writing, and especially math.

Cigarette smoking is also a widespread health hazard for the fetus and newborn. Maternal smoking is thought to cause thousands of deaths among fetuses and newborns because of placenta damage and premature births. Children of mothers who smoked during pregnancy are more likely to suffer behavioral problems later, be hyperactive, and do poorly in school. Secondhand smoke in a household where anyone is a smoker irritates a newborn's airways and is a potential cause of asthma in children.

Neonatal abstinence syndrome is a collection of problems newborns have because their pregnant mothers were using drugs that cause dependence. Those drugs get into the fetus through the placenta and cause dependence in the baby as well. When the baby is born and the drug supply ends, withdrawal reactions can show up within a few hours or not until many days later. Withdrawal can range from mild to severe, depending on the mother's usage patterns and the drug involved, and can include nervous system hyperactivity (tremors, tense muscles and exaggerated reflexes, wakefulness, seizures), digestive system dysfunction (poor feeding, vomiting, diarrhea), poor body temperature control, fever, and more. Drugs most likely to cause serious withdrawal symptoms are heroin and other opiates. However, amphetamines, barbiturates, alcohol, and even caffeine can also cause reactions.

Babies of cocaine-addicted mothers may have physical symptoms at birth that were once thought to be drug withdrawal but now are thought to be partially due to lingering effects of the drug and to poor neonatal care. In addition, many scientific studies have shown that mothers who abuse cocaine while pregnant have babies who are smaller than average, are premature more often, have more lung and other health problems, and have learning disabilities.

After a baby is born, there is still a chance that drugs will impact its development through breast milk, which contains virtually anything that is in the mother's bloodstream. A wide variety of legal drugs—prescription and over the counter—warn pregnant and nursing mothers to avoid them because of possible harm to the infant.

Contraceptives

Some women choose prescription birth control pills to prevent an unplanned pregnancy. These are taken for months or years and contain estrogens and (usually) progestins in amounts that disrupt the brain-ovary feedback loop, preventing eggs in the ovaries from maturing. But they have other effects. Birth control pills are associated with slower alcohol metabolism, so fewer drinks will have stronger effects. Women who take birth control pills and smoke are more likely to die of cardiovascular disease than those who never use the pill or smoke.

Estrogens are associated with increased risk of reproductive organ cancers, notably of the breast

117

and uterus. Estrogen-only pills were common some decades ago but were linked with thousands of cases of cancers in women. Progesterone adds protection against cancer. However, a woman needs to carefully weigh the pros and cons, in consultation with medical professionals, before using birth control pills.

Spermicides ("sperm killers") are an over-the-counter drug product, usually containing nonoxynol 9 in a gel, cream, foam, or sponge to be put into the vagina before intercourse. But they are poor contraceptives when used alone: statistics show that 18 to 26 percent of women using them will become pregnant each year.

Moreover, there are problems with spermicidal products. For some people they irritate the skin of the genitals (of both sexes), which is more than painful: it opens a route of entry for sexually transmitted pathogens. The World Health Organization (WHO) and U.S. Centers for Disease Control and Prevention have warned consumers that not only do these products not kill HIV, the virus responsible for AIDS, but they have in some studies actually increased transmission of the virus across damaged tissues. Some health organizations, especially gay men's groups, are calling for the ban of nonoxynol 9. Some manufacturers have voluntarily stopped selling it.

In the last several decades, technology has made it possible for scientists to explore the human body—from the central nervous system to the reproductive system—at the molecular and chemical levels. Scientific advances have made it possible to study an astonishingly complex array of interactions among cells and chemicals, which are constantly in flux to keep the body in a healthy state and to return it to that state after illness or injury. These discoveries have added a whole new dimension to understanding how drugs, old and new, legal and illegal, influence all body systems in both positive and negative ways.

Drug Table

COMMON NAME	CHEMICAL, GENERIC, OR BOTANICAL NAME	STREET NAMES	TYPE OF DRUG
Amphetamine, methamphetamine	(same)	Amphetamine: bennies, speed, uppers Methamphetamine: chalk, crank, crystal, crystal meth, glass, ice, meth, redneck cocaine, ya-ba	Stimulant
Benzodiazepines	Ativan, Halcion, Librium, Rohypnol, Valium, Xanax	Candy, downers, sleeping pills, tranks	Depressant
Cocaine, crack cocaine	Cocaine hydrochloride	Big C, blow, coke, candy, Charlie, crack, flake, jack, nose candy, rock, snow, whitecoat	Stimulant
Ecstasy	MDMA (3,4 methyl-enedioxymetham-phetamine)	Adam, go, hug drug, X, XTC	Stimulant/ hallucinogen
GHB	Gamma-hydroxybuty-rate	Easy lay, G, Georgia Home Boy, grievous bodily harm, gook, liquid E (or X), organic quaalude, sleep, vita-G, G juice	Depressant
Heroin (see opiates)			
Ketamine	(same)	Cat Valium, green, jet, K, kit-kat, special K, super acid, vitamin K	Dissociative
LSD	Lysergic acid diethy-lamide	Acid, California sunshine, microdot, trip, yellow sunshine	Hallucinogen

COMMON NAME	CHEMICAL, GENERIC, OR BOTANICAL NAME	STREET NAMES	TYPE OF DRUG
Marijuana	*Cannabis sativa*	Bang, blanche, blunt, dagga, dope, ganja, grass, herb, joint, pot, reefer, weed	Cannabinoid Stimulant/hallu-cinogen
Nicotine	(same)	Chewing tobacco, snuff, cigarettes, cigars, pipe tobacco	Stimulant
Opiates	Codeine, demerol, heroin, methadone, morphine, opium	Heroin: Antifreeze, big H, brown sugar, China white, gold, H, horse, mojo, smack Morphine: morf, unkie	
PCP	Phenylcyclohexylpi-peridine, phen-cyclidine	Angel dust, PeaCe pill, T	Dissociative
Ritalin	Methylphenidate	MPH, vitamin R, west coast	Stimulant
Rohypnol	Flunitrazepam	Forget-me drug, pingus, roofies, roaches, rope	Depressant (a benzodiazepine)

GLOSSARY

anabolic steroids—Types of hormones that support growth of tissues, such as muscle.

androgens—Types of steroid hormones whose actions enhance male physical and sexual characteristics.

autonomic nervous system—A group of nerves connecting the brain and many internal organs that control the body's life-supporting activities, such as heart contractions and breathing.

benzodiazepines—A group of drugs prescribed as sleeping aids, sedatives, and anti-anxiety medications.

blood-brain barrier—Specialized capillaries and adjacent cells around the brain and spinal cord that tightly restrict what substances can and cannot pass from the bloodstream into the brain and spinal cord.

capillaries—The tiniest blood vessels, carrying water, nutrients, oxygen, and other blood-borne substances, such as drugs, to every living cell.

central nervous system—The body system consisting of the brain and spinal cord, which participates in or controls virtually every aspect of physiology.

cerebral cortex—The large, most obvious portion of the human brain; the control center for complex thoughts, memories, language, awareness of sensations, control of muscles, and more.

dependence—A strong physical or psychological need for a substance.

depressant—A drug that temporarily decreases a user's physical efficiency and activity.

dopamine—A neurotransmitter strongly implicated in creating dependency to psychoactive drugs; a key participant in the pleasure circuit.

endogenous—Naturally occurring.

endorphins—Naturally occurring chemicals thought to participate in feelings of joy and well-being.

GABA—An abbreviation for gamma aminobutyric acid, a chemical that slows down some brain cell activities.

GHB—Gamma hydroxybutyrate, an anesthetic and depressant that also occurs naturally in the body; known for its abuse in sedating victims of rape.

hallucinogen—A drug that distorts a user's perceptions of reality.

homeostasis—The complex processes within a body that keep its many important substances at balanced levels.

limbic system—A group of areas within the brain involved in emotions and mood.

mechanism of action—The way in which a substance influences a cell.

medulla oblongata—The portion of the brain that connects to the spinal cord and also controls basic life-support functions, such as respiration and heartbeat.

metabolites—Chemical substances present in or formed from another chemical that affect the functioning of an organism.

neurons—Cells of the nervous system that transmit signals to other cells by a neurotransmitter.

neurotransmitters—Chemicals released by the axon of a nerve cell that influence the activities of an adjacent cell.

neurotransmitter system—A group of neurons that releases the same kind of neurotransmitter.

NSAIDs—Abbreviation for non-steroidal anti-inflammatory drugs, common over-the-counter pain relievers.

opioids—Substances that bind to opioid receptors on brain or digestive tract cells.

parasympathetic system—A network of nerves that calms and slows down the body's functions.

pathogens—Any of the several kinds of organisms, such as bacteria and viruses, that cause illness.

pleasure circuit (reward circuit)—Groups of neurons and their interconnections in the brain that respond to pleasant activities, store memories about them, and create longing to repeat them.

psychoactive drugs—The drugs that influence brain processes (thoughts, feelings, perceptions, emotions).

receptor—A specific portion of a cell's surface or its interior to which a substance binds.

route of entry—The part of the body through which a drug is taken in.

side effect—A reaction to a drug that is not part of its intended effect.

stimulant—A drug that temporarily increases a user's physical efficiency and activity.

sympathetic nervous system—That portion of the nervous system that revs up heart rate, breathing, alertness, energy use, and other properties so it can meet physical demands.

tolerance—The condition in which the body has become accustomed to the effects of a drug so that its effects are weaker and higher doses must be taken to create the original degree of response.

vasculature—The body's network of blood vessels.

withdrawal—A sign of physical dependence to a drug in which discontinuing the drug causes physical, emotional, or mental reactions as the body adjusts to the drug's absence.

NOTES

Chapter 1
p. 19, par. 3, Michael Abrams, "The Biology of Addiction: The End of Craving," *Discover,* p. 24-25.
p. 21, par. 1, Narcanon International: Drug facts and addiction help, http://www.narconon.org/druginfo/cocaine_coke.html

Chapter 2
p. 41, par. 1, Lance P. Longo and Brian Johnson, "Addiction: Part I. Benzodiazepines-Side Effects, Abuse Risk, and Alternatives," *American Family Physician,*
http://www.aafp.org/afp/20000401/2121.html
p. 42, par. 1, Dave J. Barry, Christopher B. Beach, "Barbiturate Abuse," EMedicine Consumer Health, http://www.emedicine-health.com/barbiturate_abuse/article_em.htm
p. 42, par. 2, http://science.howstuffworks.com/breathalyzer.htm
p. 48, par. 2, Igor Granta, Igor, and B. Rael Cahn, "Cannabis and Endocannabinoid Modulators: Therapeutic Promises and Challenges," *Clinical Neuroscience Research,* 5 p. 185,
http://www.cmcr.ucsd.edu/geninfo/Granta_CNR.pdf

p. 53, par. 1, National Institute on Drug Abuse, "Hallucinogens and Dissociative Drugs," http://www.drugabuse.gov/ResearchReports/Hallucinogens/halluc2.html

Chapter 3

p. 60, par. 1, Bennett Weinberg and Bonnie K. Beale, *The World of Caffeine: The Science and Culture of the World's Most Popular Drug,* p. 78.
p. 61, par. 2, Marshall Cavendish Drugs and Society series, p. 605.
p. 61, par. 3, National Institute on Drug Abuse, "Cocaine Abuse and Addiction," http://www.drugabuse.gov/ResearchReports/Cocaine/Cocaine.html

Chapter 4

p. 70, par. 2, National Institute on Drug Abuse, "Nictotine," http://www.drugabuse.gov/infofacts/nicotine.html p. 72, par. 9, National Institute on Drug Abuse, "Cocaine Abuse and Addiction," http://www.drugabuse.gov/ResearchReports/Cocaine/Cocaine.html
p. 81, par. 2, Carl E. Bartecchi, Thomas D. MacKenzie, and Robert W. Schrier, "The Human Costs of Tobacco Use," *New England Journal of Medicine,* p. 907, http://content.nejm.org/cgi/content/full/330/13/907
p. 81, par. 3, National Institute on Drug Abuse, "Nictotine," http://www.drugabuse.gov/infofacts/nicotine.html

Chapter 5

pp. 96, par. 3, Sally Fallon and Mary G. Enig, "The Long Hollow Tube: A Primer on the Digestive System," http://www.westonaprice.org/moderndiseases/digestion_primer.html
p. 97, par. 2, Igor Granta and B. Rael Cahn, "Cannabis and Endocannabinoid Modulators: Therapeutic Promises and Challenges." *Clinical Neuroscience Research,* p.185, http://www.cmcr.ucsd.edu/geninfo/Granta_CNR.pdf
p. 81, par. 2, Carl E. Bartecchi and Thomas D. MacKenzie, and Robert W. Schrier, "The Human Costs of Tobacco Use" (part 1). *New England Journal of Medicine,* 330 (March 31, 1994): 907-912. http://content.nejm.org/cgi/content/full/330/13/907

p. 101, par. 1, Gershon, Michael, *The Second Brain: A Groundbreaking New Understanding of Nervous Disorders of the Stomach and Intestine,* p. 87.

Chapter 6

p. 110, par. 3, Kuhn, Cynthia, et al, *Buzzed: The Straight Facts about the Most Used and Abused Drugs from Alcohol to Ecstasy* p. 52.

p. 114, par. 2, Henderson, L. P., C. A. Penatti, B. L. Jones, P. Yang, and A. S. Clark, "Anabolic Androgenic Steroids and Forebrain GABAergic Transmission," *Neuroscience,* p. 793, http://www.ncbi.nlm.nih.gov/entrez/query.fcgi?cmd=Retrieve&db=pubmed&dopt=Abstract&list_uids=16310317&query_hl=8&itool=pubmed_docsum

p. 117, par. 2, National Institute on Drug Abuse, "Steroids (Anabolic-Androgenic)," http://www.drugabuse.gov/infofacts/steroids.html

p. 118, par. 1, Kuhn, p. 51.

FURTHER INFORMATION

Books

Gahlinger, Paul. M. *Illegal Drugs: A Complete Guide to Their History, Chemistry, Use, and Abuse.* Salt Lake City, UT: Sagebrush Press, 2001.

Griffith, H. Winter, and Stephen Moore. *Complete Guide to Prescription and Nonprescription Drugs.* New York: Perigree Books, 2006.

Hardiman, Michael. *Overcoming Addiction: A Common Sense Approach.* Berkeley, CA: Crossing Press, 2000.

Kuhn, Cynthia, et al. *Buzzed: The Straight Facts about the Most Used and Abused Drugs from Alcohol to Ecstasy.* 2nd ed. New York: W. W. Norton & Company, 2003.

Web Sites

"The Health Consequences of Smoking: A Report of the Surgeon General" (2004). Online publication of the U.S. Department of Health and Human Services. http://www.cdc.gov/tobacco/sgr/sgr_2004/index.htm (Accessed May 11, 2006)

MedicineNet: Drug and Disease information by doctors. http://www.medicinenet.com

MedlinePlus: Information about prescription and over-the-counter drugs (sponsored by the National Library of Medicine and the National Institutes of Health). http://www.nlm.nih.gov/medlineplus/druginformation.html

Narcanon International: Drug facts and addiction help. http://www.narconon.org

National Institute on Drug Abuse for Teens: Drug information especially relevant to young people. http://www.teens.drugabuse.gov

PDR Family Guide to Over-the-Counter Drugs: Online database of information about over-the-counter drugs. http://www.pdrhealth.com/drug_info/otcdrugprofiles/alphaindexa.shtml

Sara's Quest: An interactive computer game for teens about how drugs affect the brain. National Institute on Drug Abuse. http://teens.drugabuse. gov/sarasquest/ index.asp (Accessed May 11, 2006)

BIBLIOGRAPHY

Books

Drugs and Society series. Tarrytown, NY: Marshall Cavendish, 2006.

Gershon, Michael. *The Second Brain: A Groundbreaking New Understanding of Nervous Disorders of the Stomach and Intestine.* New York: HarperCollins, 1999.

Graedon, Joe, and Teresa Graedon. *The People's Pharmacy.* NY: St. Martin's Press, 1998.

Kuhn, Cynthia, et al. *Buzzed: The Straight Facts about the Most Used and Abused Drugs from Alcohol to Ecstasy.* 2nd ed. New York: W. W. Norton & Company, 2003.

Weinberg, Bennett A., and Bonnie K. Beale. *The World of Caffeine: The Science and Culture of the World's Most Popular Drug.* New York: Routledge, 2001.

Articles

Abrams, Michael. "The Biology of Addiction: The End of Craving." *Discover,* Vol. 24, No. 5 (May 2003): 24–25.

AltMedAngel.com. "The Brain-Gut Connection."

American Academy of Pediatrics Committee on Drugs. "Neonatal Drug Withdrawal." *Pediatrics,* Vol. 101, No. 6 (June 6, 1998): 1079–1088.

American Lung Association. "Secondhand Smoke Fact Sheet" (March 2006).

Barry, Dave J., and Christopher B. Beach. "Barbiturate Abuse." EMedicine Consumer Health, http://www.emedicinehealth.com/ barbiturate_abuse/article_em.htm (Accessed May 14, 2006)

Bartecchi, Carl E., Thomas D. MacKenzie, and Robert W. Schrier. "The Human Costs of Tobacco Use" (part 1). *New England Journal of Medicine* 330 (March 31, 1994): 907–912.

Beckman, Mary. "Mary Jane Trumps Joe Camel." *Science, NOW Daily News* (May 23, 2006).

Charach, Alice, Max Figueroa, Shirley Chen, Abel Ickowicz, and Russell Schachar. "Stimulant Treatment Over 5 Years: Effects on Growth." *Journal of the American Academy of Child and Adolescent Psychiatry* 45 (April 2006): 415–421.

The Coffee Science Information Center. "Caffeine, Physical Performance and Sports."

Dubuc, Bruno. "The Brain from Top to Bottom." Canadian Institutes of Health Research, http://www.thebrain.mcgill.ca/flash/ index_d.html# (Accessed April 28, 2006)

Fleming, Mike. "Ban Called for on Nonoxynol-9 Products." October 4, 2002.

Haapanen, A., M. Koskenvuo, J. Kaprio, Y. A. Kesaniemi, and K. Heikkila. "Carotid Arteriosclerosis in Identical Twins Discordant for Cigarette Smoking." *Circulation,* Vol. 80 (1989): 10–16.

Harris, Gardiner. "F.D.A. Dismisses Medical Benefit From Marijuana." The *New York Times,* April 21, 2006.

Hartgens, F., and H. Kuipers. "Effects of Androgenic-anabolic Steroids in Athletes." *Sports Medicine,* 34 (2004): 513-554.

Henderson, L. P., C. A. Penatti, B. L. Jones, P. Yang, and A. S. Clark. "Anabolic Androgenic Steroids and Forebrain GABAergic Transmission." *Neuroscience,* 138 (2006): 793–799. http:// science.howstuffworks.com/breathalyzer.htm

Leshner, A. I., and G. F. Koob. "Drugs of Abuse and the Brain." Proceedings of the Association of American Physicians 111 (Mar–Apr 1999): 99–108.

Longo, Lance P., and Brian Johnson. "Addiction: Part I. Benzodiazepines-Side Effects, Abuse Risk, and Alternatives." *American Family Physician,* Vol. 61, No. 7 (April 1, 2000): 2121–2130.

Massa, F., et al. "The Endogenous Cannabinoid System Protects Against Colonic Inflammation." *Journal of Clinical Investigation,* Vol. 113, No. 8 (April 2004): 1202–1209.

Mohsenifar, Zab. "Chronic Obstructive Pulmonary Disease (COPD)." MedicineNet.com

National Institute on Drug Abuse. "Cocaine Abuse and Addiction." NIH Publication No. 99–4342 (November 2004). http://www.drugabuse.gov/ResearchReports/Cocaine/Cocaine.html (Accessed April 28, 2006)

National Institute on Drug Abuse. "Hallucinogens and Dissociative Drugs." NIH Publication No. 01–4209 (February 2001) http://www.drugabuse.gov/ResearchReports/Hallucinogens/halluc2.html (Accessed April 28, 2006)

National Institute on Drug Abuse. "Heroin Abuse and Addiction." NIH Publication No. 05–4165 (May 2005). http://www.drugabuse.gov/ResearchReports/Heroin/Heroin.html (Accessed April 28, 2006)

National Institute on Drug Abuse. "Inhalant Abuse." NIH Publication No. 00-3818 (2005). http://www.drugabuse.gov/ResearchReports/Inhalants/Inhalants.html (Accessed April 28, 2006)

National Institute on Drug Abuse. "Marijuana." http://www.nida.nih.gov/Infofacts/marijuana.html (Accessed April 27, 2006)

National Institute on Drug Abuse. "MDMA Abuse (Ecstasy)." NIH Publication No. 05-4728 (November 2005). http://www.drugabuse.gov/ResearchReports/MDMA/default.html (Accessed April 28, 2006)

National Institute on Drug Abuse. "Methamphetamine Abuse and Addiction." NIH Publication No. 02-4210 (April 1998). http://teens.drugabuse.gov/mom/tg_meth2.asp (Accessed April 14, 2006)

National Institute on Drug Abuse for Teens. "Methamphetamine: Mechanism of Action." (November 29, 2005). http://www.drugabuse.gov/ResearchReports/methamph/methamph2.html#what (Accessed April 28, 2006)

National Institute on Drug Abuse. "Nictotine." http://www.drugabuse.gov/ResearchReports/Nicotine/Nicotine.html (Accessed April 28, 2006)

National Institute on Drug Abuse. "Steroids (Anabolic-Androgenic)." http://www.drugabuse.gov/infofacts/steroids.html (Accessed April 28, 2006)

National Institute on Drug Abuse for Teens. "Stimulants: Mechanism of Action" (November 29, 2005). http://teens.drugabuse.gov/mom/tg_stim2.asp (Accessed April 14, 2006)

National Institute on Drug Abuse. "Tobacco Addiction." NIH Publication No. 06-4342 (1998). http://www.drugabuse.gov/ResearchReports/Nicotine/Nicotine.html (Accessed April 28, 2006)

Nestler, Eric J., and Robert C. Malenka. "The Addicted Brain." ScientificAmerican.com (February 9, 2004). "Over-the-counter Birth Control." MedlinePlus Medical Dictionary. (Updated May 15, 2006) http://www.nlm.nih.gov/medlineplus/ency/article/004003.htm (Accessed April 28, 2006)

Seaman, Barbara. *The Greatest Experiment Ever Performed on Women: Exploding the Estrogen Myth.* New York: Hyperion, 2003.

Standridge, John B., Robert G. Zylstra, and Stephen M. Adams. "Alcohol Consumption: An Overview of Benefits and Risks." Southern Medical Journal 97 (2004): 664-672. http://www.ncbi.nlm.nih.gov/entrez/query.fcgi?cmd=Retrieve&db=PubMed&list_uids=15301124&dopt=Abstract (Accessed May 8, 2006)

Stöppler, Melissa C. "Steroid Abuse." MedicineNet.com, http://www.medicinenet.com/script/main/art.asp?articlekey=52945 (Accessed May 21, 2006)

United States Department of Health and Human Services. "The Health Consequences of Smoking: A Report of the Surgeon General" (2004). http://www.cdc.gov/tobacco/sgr/sgr_2004/index.htm (Accessed May 11, 2006)

Weinberg, Bennett A., and Bonnie K. Beale. *The World of Caffeine: The Science and Culture of the World's Most Popular Drug.* New York: Routledge, 2001.

INDEX

Page numbers in **boldface** are illustrations, tables, and charts.

acetaminophen, 100
acetylcholine (ACh), 33, 38, 41
acid reflux, 88, 97, 98, 100-102
acne, 8, 113
addiction, 83, 84–86, 90, 96
addictive substances, 15-17, 38, 77, 92, 110
additives, caffeine, 38–39
adduct, 80
adenosine, 39, 50, 54, 55, 96
adrenals, 107–108
adverse effects, 22–23, 98, **99**, 124
age, 15, 81, 98, **104**, 109, 114–117

aggression, 45, 50-51, 111, 114
AIDS, 48, 97, 118-119
airways, 69–72, 75, 77–85, **77**, 116
alcohol, 7, 10, 15-17, 26, 28, 33, 39–41, 42, 43, 61–63, 65, 70, 73–76, 94, 108–110, 115–117, 118
alcoholic hepatitis, 95
allergens, 30, 85
allergic reactions to drugs, 23–25, 30, 72, **99**
allergy medications, 8, 28-30, 40, 52, 70, 84
alveoli, 69, 71, 78, 79, 83

amphetamines, 9, 11, 16, 35–36, 58, 72, 91–92, 109, 117, **120**

amygdala, 19, **19**

anabolic steroids, 11, 50–52, **104**, 111–114, **112**, 122

anaphylactic shock, 24

androgens, 50–51, 106–108, 111–113, **112**, 122

anesthetics, 9, 47, 49, 65, 70, 73–76

anoxia, 62

antidepressants, 10, 17, 30, 43–45, 106, 108, 115

antihistamines, 20, 40, 52, 84–85

anxiety, 17, 39-42, 48, 62, 75

appetite, 34, 37, 44–45, 47–48, 90–95, 97, 100–102

arteriosclerosis, 59, 60, 62

artificial sweeteners, 23

asphyxiation, 75

aspirin, 52, 56, 67, 100

asthma, 72, 73, 81, 85, 116

Ativan, 41–42

attention deficit hyperactivity disorder (ADHD), 35, 37, 58, 116

attentiveness, 10, 37, 39, 64

autonomic nervous system, 87, 122

axons, 18, 19, 31

bacterial pathogens, 10, 57-58, 75, 78, 82, 85, 97, 103

barbiturates, 22, 61, 75, 76, 117

behavior changes, 10, 47, 50–51

benzene, 65

benzodiazepines, 17, 22, 40–43, 61–62, 75–76, **120–121**, 122

bilirubin, 95

binge drinking, 74–75

birth control drugs, **104**, 105–106, 108, 117–119

blood-brain barrier, 10, **29**, 75–76, 122

blood pressure, 50, 58, 59, 60, 63–67, 88–91, 113–114

bloodstream, 7–10, 14, 23, 44, 50, 55–58, 60, 62–63, 67

over-the-counter drugs and, 67, 84, 102

reproductive system and, 106–107, **112**

blood vessels, 8, **54**, 55–59, 61, 63, 65–67, **66**, 89, 100

body-building enhancers, 39, 43, 56, 72, 76, 112-113, **112**

brain, 8, 10-13, 16, 18–19, **19**, 27–31, **29**, 33, 39, 40,` 49–51, 55–56, 58, 61–65, 72–76, 88–95, 100, 101, 107–117 brain damage, from drugs, 53, 58, 59, 62, 74, 115–117

brainstem, 28-31, **29**, 40

Breathalyzer test, 42

breathing, 22, 24, 28, 40, 43, 45, **68**, 70, 72–74, 76, 79, 81, 83, 85, 110

bronchi, 69, 78

bronchioles, 69, 73, 78–79, 83–85

bronchitis, 78, 81

bronchodilator drugs, 85

butane, 49

caffeine, 17, 20, 26, 33, 35, 38–39, 53, 58–60, 72–73, 94, 98, 109, 117

    withdrawal symptoms, 117

calcium ions, 38

cancers, 48, 64, 71, 77, 79–81, 97, 118

carbon monoxide, 77, 80–81

cardiovascular system, **6**, **54**, 55–67, 59–60, **66**, 72, 118

central nervous system, 11, **26**, 27–53, **29**, **32**, 41, 56, 65, 69, 85, 90, 116–117

cerebral cortex, 19, **29**, 30–31, 123

chewing tobacco, 8, 9, 38, 79, 80, **121**

cigarettes/cigars, 8, 9, 69–71, 77–82, 93, 116, **121**

cilia, 78

cirrhosis of liver, 62, 95

clotting of blood, 56, 60–61, 67

club drugs, 70

cocaine, 8–9, 11, **12**, 16–17, 21, 22, 52, 56, 58, 71–72, 92–93, 109–110. *See also* stimulants.

codeine, 45–46, 52

coffee, 38–39, 73, 94

cold/flu medications, 20, 28–29, 40, 46, 52, 81, 84

coma, 43, 50, 59, 62, 74

constipation, 88, 96, 98, 102–103

contraceptive drugs. *See* Birth control drugs.

coughing, 23, 28–30, 79, 84

cough medications, 7, 20, 84–85

crack cocaine, names for, **120**

"crash" phase, 33

cravings, 17, 44–47, 93

Crohn's disease, 97

"date rape" drugs, 39, 42–43, 110, 123

death, 16, 50, 59, 62, 65, 70, 74, 76, 78–80, 83, 103

dependence, 123

    drugs causing, 15–21, 33, 42, 45–46, 92–93, 116–117

depressants, 10, 22, 28, 35, 39–41, 42, 45–46, 48, 52, 56, 60–62, 63, 65, 73–75, 85, 108, 110, 123

depression, 30, 43, 45, 51, 115

detoxifying, 8, 13, 35, 61, 89

diarrhea, 21, 88, 98, 102–103

dieting, 90–94

digestive aids, 98-100, **99**

digestive tract, **6**, 21–22, 49, 67, 75, **86**, 87–103, 116–117

dissociatives, 46–48, 114–115

dopamine, 11–12, 18–20, **32**, 33–38, 44, 46–47, 48, 88, 91–93

drug interactions, 22, 67, **99**

drugs of abuse, 20, 33–35, 37, 43, 47, 76, 88, 90

eating disorders, 44–45

Ecstasy (MDMA), 35, 47, **120**

emergency room medications, 29

emerging medical treatment, 24–25, 100

emphysema, 78-79

endogenous cannabinoids, 49, 63–64, 96–97, 101

endogenous opiates, 33–34, 45–46, 75, 88, 96, 101

endorphins, 11, 34, 96, 123

energy drinks, 38–39, 73, 109

entry routes for drugs, 8–9, 57–58, 71–72, 83, **86**, 88–90, 124

epinephrine, 34, 91

estrogens, 106-108, 113, 117–118

euphoria, 21, 33, 37, 48, 49

eustachian tubes, 81–82

fat cells and molecules, 14, 90–91

fentanyl, 16, 45–46, 61. *See also* opiates.

fetal alcohol effects, 116

fetal alcohol syndrome, 115

Food and Drug Administration (FDA), 17, 20

Framingham Heart Study, 60

GABA (gamma-aminobutyric acid), 21, 33, 41, 43, 46, 51–52, 74, 76

gastroesophageal reflux disease, 88, 97–98, 100–102

genetic disorders, 107–108

genitalia, external, 106–108, 118

genital warts, 109

GHB (gamma-hydroxybutyric acid), 22, 39, 43, 61, 73–74, 76, 110, **120**, 123

hallucinogens, 10, 14, 16–17, 46–49, 114–115, 123

heart, 28–29, 55, 58–63, 65, **66**

heart attack, 23, 62, 64–65, 67, 89, 102

heartbeat (rate), 22, 30–31, 33, 60, 62–65, 67, 85, 110

heartburn, 88, 97–98, 100–102

hepatitis, 57, 95, 108, 109

herbal products, 67, 108–109

heroin, 9, 11, 13, 16–17, 20, 22, 33, 61, 73–74, 108, 116–117

45–46. *See also* opiates.
herpes, 109
HIV (human immunodeficiency virus), 57, 108, 109, 118
homeostasis, 21, 24, 123
hyperactivity, 21, 35, 37, 58, 116

ibuprofen, 52
illegal drugs, 7, 9, 15, 33-36, 39–41, 55–58, 64, **68**, 86, 108, 112
illicit drugs, 12, 15, 26, 28, 30, 56–57, 88–89
infant, 98, **104**, 109, 115–117
inhalants, 17, 49–50, 65–67, **66**, 69–71, 83–84, 114–115
inhaling, 8–9, 70, 71, 79, 81–82, 85, 92
injection, 9, 37, 43, 57, 90, 92
  anabolic steroids, 112, **112**
  illegal drugs, 9, 57–58, 93, 109–110
insomnia, 17, 21, 41–42, 76
intestines, 8–9, 88–91, 101–103
intravenous injection, 9, 57, 75

ketamine, 43, 47, 48, 110, **120**
kidneys, 13–15, 23, 80, 113
Klonopin, 41–42, 43

laxatives, 103
learning disabilities, 64, 115–117

legal drugs, 7–9, 15, 26, 39–41, **68**, 86
life-support systems of body, 28
limbic system, 29–30, **29**, 31, 123
lipids, 14, 113–114
liver, 13, 15, 23, 62, 91–95, 97
  damage to, 94–95, 97–98, 113
LSD, 17, 47, **120**
lungs, 8–9, 69–73, 75, **77**, 78–85

malnutrition, 93–95
manufacturers of legal drugs, 15, **99**, 128–129
MAOIs (monoamine oxidase inhibitors), 44
marijuana, 8, 11, 17, 33, 43, 48–49, 63–64, 70–71, 80–83, 114–115, **121**
maté, 38–39
mechanism of action, 10–12, 123
medulla oblongata, 28, **29**, 123
memories, 29–30, 40, 48, 64
mental processes, 7, 10, 16, 37, 43
mescaline, 17, 47
mesolimbic dopamine pathway, 18
metabolism of drugs, 15, 95, 97–98, 113, 118

metabolites, 13–14, **14**, 97, 123

methamphetamine, 12, 35–37, 71, 90, **120**

methanol, 65

methylphenidate, 35

methylxanthines, 39, 72–73

mimicking of drugs, 10, 20, 36, 46, 53, 59, 75, 88, 91, 95, **104**

monoamine oxidase, 44

mood, 10–11, 17, 29-30, 43–44, 47, 49–51, 114

morphine, 9, 11, 13, 16, 45–46, 61, 73–75, 96

See also opiates.

motor neurons, 28

motor outputs, 19, **19**

mouth, 8, 69, 78–80, 82, 89, 92

muscle aches, 21, 24

muscle coordination, 9, 28, 33–34, 49, 115

muscle movements, 30, 40, 72–73, 76

muscle strength/weakness, 24, 40, 43, 49, 64, 111–114, **112**

muscular reflexes, 30, 76

nasal sprays, 8, 20, 84–85

naturopathic remedy, 22

nausea, 15–16, 23, 29, 48, 64, 75, 83

digestive tract/drugs, 88, 96, 98

neonatal abstinence syndrome, 116

nerve cells, 14, 18–19, 101

toluene effects on, 50

nervous system, **6**

neurobiologists, 18–19, 28, 31, 49

neurochemical changes, 12

neurological syndromes, 50

neurons, 12–13, 16, 18–19, 24, 28-29, 31–33, **32**

antidepressants' actions on, 44

cardiovascular system, 55–56, 59

dopamine, 11–12, 37, 46

GABA effect on activities, 41, 74, 76

hallucinogens' and dissociatives'effects, 48

marijuana effects on, 49

opiates' effects on, 46

pain sensation, 100

stimulants and, 36, 39

neurotransmitters, 18, 24, 31–36, **32**, 38, 45, 123

antidepressants' effects on, 44

cocaine effects, 93

digestive tract and, 92, 101

hallucinogens and, 47

monoamine, 43-44

opiates' actions on, 46

neurotransmitter system, 41, 43, 51–52, 123

depressant effects on, 40, 41, 74

dissociative drugs' effects, 48

nicotine, 8–9, 16–17, 26, 30–31, 35, 38, 60–61, 69–70, 72, 77–82, **77**, 89, **121**

nicotinic receptors, 38

nitric oxide, 89

nitrous oxide, 49, 65

NMDA receptors, 48

nociceptors, 52

nonoxynol 9, 118–119

norepinephrine, 33, 35–36, 44, 47–48, 91, 93

nose, 8–9, 69, 84–85

NSAIDs (nonsteroidal anti-inflammatory drugs), 52, 100, 124

nucleus accumbens, 18–19, **19**

nutritional supplements, 22

opiates (opioids), 11, 16–17, 20–21, 40, 45–46, 61, 73–75, 9, 116–117, **121**

oral ingestion, 8, 9, 28, 37, 75, 87–88, 90, 112, **112**

ovaries, 106–107, 117

overdose, 15, 20, 42, 60, 76, 83

alcohol, 61–62

liver damage and, 98

over-the-counter drugs, 17, 20, 22, 25, 28, 46, 52–53, 56,

67, 70, 84–85, 98–99, **99**, 118

pain, 11, 48, 52, 79, 84, 88–89

abdominal, 15–16, 98–99

as allergic reaction, 23

pain relievers, 8–9, 16–17, 20, 45–46, 52–53, 56, 75

digestive tract and, 96, 100

nonprescription, 100

Paxil, 115

PCP (phencyclidine), 14, 47, 48, 53, 71, **121**

perception of reality, 10, 30, 40, 45–49, 74, 114-115

peristalsis, 96, 101, 103

Physician's Desk Reference, 23

pleasure circuit, 11–12, 16, 18–19, **19**, 33, 36, 38, 88, 92, 93, 124

pregnancy/nursing, 108–110, 114–117

premenstrual mood changes, 44–45

prescription drugs, 15, 22–23, 28–30, 37, 40–45, 56–58, 62, 64, 67, **78**, 75–76, 89–90, 98, **99**, 108, 111–112, 117–119

progesterone, 118

progestins, 106–107, 117

prostaglandins, 52, 100

protein, 12, 31

Prozac, 44, 115

psilocybin, 47
psychoactive drugs, 10–14,
33–34, 48, 53, 88, 89, 106,
108, 124
puberty, 105–107, 114

rash, 8, 23–24
receptor, 12–13, 20, 31, **32**, 41,
48–49, 124
opiates and, 21–22, 46
receptor down-regulation, 20
receptor-steroid complex, 51
relaxation, 40, 45, 48, 70
before surgery, 42
reproductive system, **6**, **104**,
105–119, **112**
respiratory system, **6**, **68**,
69–85, **77**
Ritalin, 35, 37, 58, **121**
Rohypnol, 39, 43, 110, **121**
rush, 9, 33

seasonal affective disorder,
44–45
sedatives, 39–41, 62, 75–76,
110
seizures, 16, 23, 42, 50, 59, 62
sensory neurons, 28

sensory perceptions, 18–20,
19, 47, 49
septum, **19**
serotonin, 33–36, 41, 44, 47,
88, 92, 107, 115

sexual behavior, 18, 21, 47,
50–52, 109–111, 114–115
sleepiness, daytime, 17, 39–40,
45, 48, 75–76
sleeping pills, 8, 22, 39–41, 62
slurred speech, 10, 40, 49
smoking
cessation aids, 8, 35, 61, 89
cigarettes, 8–9, 31, 38, 43,
59–61, 118
of cocaine, 9, 93
digestive tract and, 93
marijuana, 71, 80–83
nonsmokers' risk, 61, 78,
80–82, 116
respiratory system and,
69–72, 77–82, **77**, 85
sneezing, 28–30
sniffing, 8, 9, 65, 71
snorting, 8, 9, 37, 71, 90,
92–93, 109–110
snuff, 79, **121**
spermicides, 118
spinal cord, 28, 45
SSRIs (selective serotonin reuptake inhibitors), 44–45, 115
steroid-based drugs,
107–108, 111–114, **112**
steroid hormones, 50-52,
105–109, 111–114
stimulants, 10, 12, 14, 22, 24,
28, 34–39, 48, 53, 56,
58–60, 70, 72–75, 90–91,
93–94, 106, 108–110

street "laced" drugs, 57–58

stress, 70

stroke, 59, 62, 67

sudden infant death syndrome (SIDS), 82

sudden sniffing death syndrome, 65

suicide, 45, 76

sympathetic nervous system, 34–35, 56, 58–60, 63, 65, 70, 90–91, 124

stimulants and, 90–91

testes, 106, 107, 113

testosterone, 111–113, **112**

THC (delta-9-tetrahydro-cannabinol), 11, 48–49, 63–64, 96–97

theobromine, 39

theophylline, 39, 72–73

throat, 71, 78, 81–82, 84

tobacco, 8–9, 15, 38, 43, 60–61, 70, 77–82, **77**, **121**

tolerance, 20–21, 124

toluene, 49–50, 65, 70

toxins, 10, 21, 71, 80, 82, 97

trachea, 69, 78

tranquilizers, 39–41

transporter proteins, 36, 37

treatment plans, drug users, 11

tryptamine drugs, 47

tumors, steroid-producing, 107–108

ulcers, 97

unconsciousness, 43, 62, 74–76

urine tests, **14**

uterus, 106–107

Valium, 41–42

vasculature, 8, 124

ventral tegmental area (VTA), 18–19, **19**

veterinary products, 112

viruses, 10, 78, 85, 97, 103

vomiting, 15–16, 21, 28–29, 64, 75, 83

warning labels, 40, 45, 52, 85, 98, **99**, 117

water-soluble drugs, 14

weight loss, 48, 64

withdrawal, defined, 124

withdrawal symptoms, 15–17, 21–22, 42, 11–117

Xanax, 41–43

Zoloft, 44, 115

ABOUT THE AUTHOR

Lorrie Klosterman, Ph.D., is a biologist and a freelance writer and educator. Her books for Marshall Cavendish Benchmark include *Leukemia, Meningitis, The Facts About Caffeine,* and *The Facts About Depressants.*